# Organizing Her Life

## *Laura Souders*

# Organizing Her Life

healthier spaces
organizing

# Laura Souders

*"Is it time to consciously create YOUR life? ORGANIZING HER LIFE is a combination of a good beach novel, a how to get organized guide, and a follow your dreams self-help book - I loved it! Laura humanizes organizing giving just enough information that the reader can absorb it but not so much that they get overwhelmed and bogged down. Mixing inspiration and her own family story that I certainly could identify with – I just couldn't wait to read more."*

Ellen Faye, COC®, CPO ®

Productivity and Leadership Coach | Certified Organizer Coach® | Certified Professional Organizer®

**Past President: National Association of Productivity and Organizing Professionals (NAPO)**


*"When I started Feel Your Boobies®, I had been diagnosed with breast cancer and had a life altering experience. I didn't want to waste time, I wanted to provide young women with the knowledge to feel their boobies and be the first line of defense against breast cancer. Through breast cancer I found my passion and purpose. In Organizing Her Life, Laura explains how she found her passion and purpose and the obstacles that were in the way of finding true happiness. Her story will motivate you to wake up and make the changes you want in your life today."*

Leigh Hurst

Founder/Executive Director

**Feel Your Boobies® Foundation**

# Organizing Her Life

*How My Journey Can Help
You Declutter Your Spaces
and Your Life*

**Laura Souders**

*I would like to dedicate this book to my husband and children.*

*Scott: You agreed to go on this journey with me and have never looked back. Thank you for your unwavering support and encouragement, it speaks volumes.*

*Natalie, Zach, and Ryan: Each one of you possesses unique gifts and talents. As you are becoming adults and figuring out what makes your heart sing, I want you to remember to always be true to yourself.*

# Table of Contents

# *Introduction*

In our current culture, people are weighed down with a tremendous amount of physical and mental clutter. The excess makes us feel overwhelmed, stressed, and trapped. In *Organizing Her Life*, you'll learn how to use the unique system I created: Set Goals, Purge, Conscious Placement, and Maintenance. I developed this system as a tool to help my clients organize their homes and found it beneficial in other areas of life. These four steps will show you how to uncover your goals, eliminate what isn't useful, consciously reorganize, and develop methods to maintain your progress. Tips and prompts are provided throughout the book for personal reflection and application.

As a member of the National Association of Productivity and Organizing Professionals (NAPO) since 2014, I have watched as my clients' lives have been transformed through organization. As people let go of things they no longer need, they feel lighter and often exclaim, "I can breathe again." They have more time and energy available to propel their lives in a new direction, maybe deciding to eat healthy, pursue a new career, or sell a home. I notice in the absence of clutter, an awareness arose. I believe that by simplifying our homes and spaces, it is easier to follow the path we desire.

I wrote *Organizing Her Life* to explain how I personally applied this process to my life. I arranged the book into my four-step structure, so you can see how I evaluated my life, purged the things that no longer fulfilled me, and redesigned my life. I experienced amazing results that I believe can be achieved by anyone who is ready to take the journey.

After reading this book, you will reconsider the clutter in your life, whether physical or mental, and be inspired to make a change. Start now. Don't wait one more day to take the steps to create your perfect life.

*Laura Souders*

Owner of Healthier Spaces Organizing

# GOALS

What is the vision you have for your space? Often, people say, "I just want it organized." This is too vague. What will *organized* look like to you? Imagine we are talking about a kitchen. Does organized mean that there will be nothing on the countertops? It does to some people. Others want all of their appliances close at hand and would feel like the space was bare without decorations on the countertop. How will your space look? How do you want to feel in your space? What do you want to do in the space? Your goal will be unique to you. If you don't set a goal, you won't know exactly what you are working toward.

# CHAPTER ONE

# *Acknowledge the Problem*

Become aware of your space, and recognize when it
no longer works for you.

Every August, my goal was always the same: make it
to June. One hundred and eighty days felt like an
eternity when I was teaching 1st grade. I sat down at
my desk and sighed deeply. The room smelled
faintly of disinfectant wipes and Cheez-it crackers
from snack time. I knew the next thirty minutes of
solitude would go by too quickly. It was afternoon
Music Class time, one of the rare moments in the day
when my room didn't contain twenty kids full of
unlimited energy. I scanned my desk with its
organized containers of pencils and pens sitting
beside end-of-the-year gifts children had given to me
over the years. Facing the classroom at the front edge
of my desk, there was a yellow wooden name plate
in the shape of a pencil: Mrs. Souders. To the right
were three bells: a small apple-shaped bell, a cow

bell, and a large shiny bell because I learned years ago that new sounds grabbed the students' attention.

On the other side of my desk was a black and white picture of Scott and me from our wedding— the exact day I became Mrs. Souders. We looked young and in love. Next to it, sat a picture I took of our kids for a Christmas card several years ago. I had given each of them a huge swirled lollipop that practically covered their faces. Their smiles were enormous. When I first started teaching almost seventeen years ago, my desk was nearly empty with only a stack of teaching manuals and the activities I needed for the week. *I was supposed to leave years ago. Why was I still here?*

I looked at the miniature desks and chairs in groups of four. The chores had been forgotten—the bookshelf needed straightening, the trash can was overflowing, and pencil shavings lay in a pile by the sharpener. The front of the room was decorated with a colorful calendar and job chart trimmed in coordinating sparkly borders. A long alphabet chart hung above the length of the stained white board. Laminated signs posted around the room assigned areas for the children to read quietly, paint, have computer time, or make a lunch selection. An oversized, fuzzy, purple, stuffed crayon and huge plastic pencil were suspended from the ceiling in front of a window. I remember how excited I had been to get the pencil from a department store that was going out of business and how thrilled the students were when they walked into the room the day I hung it. Now, I noticed it looked faded, and a layer of dust had settled on it.

"Hey, Laura." Leslie, my next-door teaching neighbor, walked into the room holding papers. "I brought you these math games you can use for practicing adding and subtracting."

"Thanks," I said as Leslie handed me the papers, but she didn't let go of the stack.

"Here. Let me explain it to you. It's a chart, and then the kids…"

As soon as she said "chart" I realized I hadn't finished my lesson plans for next week and would have to take them home to do over the weekend.

"…sounds fun, right?" Leslie was excited for my kids to try the game. I was sure that they'd love it too, but I couldn't match her excitement right then. It was Friday, and I was drained.

"Confetti time?" I walked over to the table shaped like a half moon, and Leslie slid out a miniature student size chair. I pulled a large plastic bucket of confetti off the window ledge.

The bucket of confetti was a free gift I ordered from a magazine company, along with stickers and an electronic bell that had six different sounds. There were more than ten different categories, including Christmas trees, four-leaf clovers, pumpkins, music notes, and cats, but when I ordered the confetti, I didn't realize it would be a jumbled mixture. When would I ever use all of those things in one project? The bucket sat for a full year in my art supply cupboard next to the glitter and glue. It bothered me that it was unused and taking up so much space. I thought maybe if I separated it into groups of similar items, I might find a project to use it. At the beginning of the school year, I started sorting the tightly packed bucket while the students were out of the room at a special class. I found it calming to take a handful of the chaotic confetti and turn it into organized little piles.

"It's our turn for staff breakfast next Friday," I reminded Leslie. I had written all the special days in my plan book because I didn't want to miss a treat day or a chance to wear jeans to school.

Once a month, each grade level took turns and provided breakfast for the staff. I craved the thirty minutes of adult conversation that happened at these gatherings. The time flew by quickly, and before I was ready, the morning bell rang, sending everyone scurrying to their classrooms.

"That's right! I was thinking it would be fun to have a theme this time," Leslie said as Amy, another teacher in our hallway, walked in.

"A theme for what? Oh my gosh! Are you guys sorting again?" said Amy, teasing. Laughing, she pulled up a child-size chair and scooped out a handful of glittery shapes.

"It's our turn for staff breakfast next Friday, and we were just talking about having a theme. What do you think?" I asked.

"Oh, since we teach 1st grade, how about an apple theme with apple juice, hot apple cider, cinnamon apple muffins, and Applewood bacon?" Amy loved the opportunity to be creative.

We decided who would bring each item. I planned on making a baked oatmeal and bringing apple cider. I walked over to my desk to write down a reminder of my contributions and glanced at the large clock on the wall.

"It's 3:15. Time to get the kids from specials," I told Leslie and Amy.

They pushed each of their small sorted mounds into mine. I slid each large pile off the table and into separate lidded containers.

I was ready for the week to be over, but I hadn't finish planning my lessons for next week. I would have to take work home. I shoved my plan book and two oversized teaching manuals into my school bag. The task of planning would hang over my head the whole weekend.

Every Sunday during the school year, I woke up with a feeling of dread that continued to build throughout the day. By the evening, the gloomy emptiness weighed heavily on me. I didn't mind the process of planning. Actually, I enjoyed choosing the activities I would use for each lesson, figuring out how long they would take, and writing the materials and plans in the little daily blocks. The Sunday dread stemmed from the realization that I was planning away another five days of my life. Week by week, my life was slowly ticking by. Being in the classroom was not something I enjoyed, and each day, there was another day that I wasn't with my own children. By the time I finished writing plans on

Sunday, it would be past 8 o'clock, my own kids would be getting ready for bed, and the usual fights about brushing teeth would ensue.

As the school day came to an end, I went to the Music room and led my students through the school to the courtyard for dismissal. On the way, we passed the classroom of a first-year teacher. She was lining up her class and singing a goodbye song. It was easy to spot the new teachers in a building. They were the energetic, optimistic ones with the "I am going to change the world" attitude.

I remember when I was hired for my first teaching job right out of college. I studied teaching manuals on family vacations, labored over which color of paper to use for each bulletin board, and made fun review games: coloring, cutting, and laminating each piece. I wanted to make everything perfect for my students.

Initially, I had been hired as a temporary employee. My parents both spent their whole careers in the public school system, so I knew how competitive the job market was with few positions available each year. It was important to set myself apart from the other applicants. To increase my chances of a permanent job, I accepted additional coaching positions throughout the year. All the after-school activities added to my already busy first year of teaching, but the extra effort paid off.

When the head of Human Resources called to offer me a job, he said, "*I have a full-time, permanent position to offer you.*"

I immediately answered, "*I'll take it.*"

"*You might want to wait until I explain the position. It's…different.*"

But I knew no matter what he said, I was going to accept the offer. I had decided as soon as I heard "full-time" and "permanent." Scott and I were getting married in five days, and I desperately wanted a secure job.

The head of Human Resources continued, describing that I would be in two different classrooms. In the morning, I would teach reading at the middle school, and then in the afternoon, I would teach a kindergarten class.

"*Thank you so much!*" I accepted the job as a foot in the door. I could do anything for a year.

That next school year was challenging. In many aspects, I had double the amount of work: lesson plans, report cards, parent–teacher conferences, and two very different groups of students. I left home each day dressed in a suit and heels to teach hormonal 7th and 8th graders who would rather be anywhere than at school. I taught four classes at the middle school, and then I hopped in my little red Honda at lunchtime and drove to my kindergarten session. I loved driving with the moon roof open and feeling the sun shining on me. I was out while everyone else was stuck in a building.

Before I walked into the elementary school, I did a quick "costume change" in the parking lot. I replaced my blazer with a cardigan sweater, changed into flat shoes, and put on a large school bus or seasonal pin. The five-year-olds were so happy to be at school. I looked forward to their attitude when I left the middle school.

I tried to make the best of the year, but I felt run down. I had eight sinus infections that year. It was only my second year of teaching, but I clearly remember wondering how many years I would have to teach before I could retire.

The following year, I was relieved to be able to transfer to a third grade classroom. Being at one building, I wouldn't have to rush from one class to the next, change outfits in the car, or do lesson planning for two grade levels. Although I had more time to work in my room, I often sat at my desk, staring out the windows. I longed for the opportunity to leave each day. Doubts about being a teacher crept in my thoughts that year for the very first time, and they remained every year after, regardless of grade level or building assignment.

As I watched the new teacher sing her kids a goodbye song, all I could think about were how many days I had left until summer.

---

*Life is short. Wishing things were different won't change them. You need to make a plan for change to occur. Be an active participant in your life. The first step is to choose what you want to pursue.*

- *What do you wish could change in your life?*
- *What could you do to change it?*

---

CHAPTER TWO

# *Be Willing to Ask for Help*

Whether it is a friend, family member, or a
professional,
there is someone you can call on for help.

The first week of summer vacation, I woke up early
before the kids. There were strawberries growing in
our gardens for another few days, and I was eager to
pick some for breakfast. I didn't bother to change out
of my pajama shorts and tank top because I would
only be out for a few minutes. I grabbed a large
plastic bowl and quietly slid open the back porch
door.

Usually, I would walk around outside bare
foot, but the grass was still a little wet from the
morning dew. So, I slipped into flip-flops. I breathed
in the fresh air as I walked out to a patch on the side
of our house that got the best sun. I stepped into the
damp dirt, landing on a mushy, rotten berry.

I couched down, pulling the deep red berries off the plant. My fingers quickly became stained from the juice. I alternated putting them in the bowl and popping them into my mouth, not waiting to wash them, sampling to see if the darker red ones were sweeter than the others. They would be perfect for strawberry shortcake. I felt light and relaxed, living in the moment. The pressure to pretend to be someone else had been lifted off me like a heavy weight for the next few months. I longed to feel like this every day.

I quickly filled the bowl and got another one. When I walked back outside, I was distracted. This was the first time I had a chance to survey my garden. I wanted to see if the basil seeds we planted were growing, if the tomato plants needed guiding in their cages, and how our two new raspberry bushes were doing.

I saw some weeds and bent down to pick them. It felt so good to get my hands in the dirt and rip out the uninvited plants. I saw a few more and moved over to yank them out. *I'll just pull ten more weeds,* I promised myself.

Scott opened the sliding glass door, dressed in a t-shirt and tan shorts. "Do the kids have swim team practice this morning?"

Startled, I answered, "Yeah. I'm coming in soon. Can you wake everyone up before you leave for class?"

I wasn't used to Scott's new schedule or seeing him dressed like this. For over ten years, Scott had been working with his dad at their successful home building business. They built several of the houses in our neighborhood, including the house we lived in. Scott left each morning wearing an old t-shirt, carpenter jeans, and heavy-duty boots. Summer was the best season for building in Pennsylvania. The weather was warm and dry, and the days were long. He worked long days in the summer.

When the housing market took a sudden dive, Scott had a lot of extra time. He wanted to do something meaningful and to benefit our community. He had played football in high school and college, so he returned as an assistant coach at Middletown, helping the program that had supported him. We called the night before football practices started, "his Christmas eve." His excitement was unmistakable. I loved seeing him joyful and content.

While he was at the high school for practices, he heard about an hourly position running the In-School Suspension room. Scott decided to take the job as a good way to get to know the high school kids. It would be temporary until business picked up.

When home building didn't pick up, Scott and his dad closed the business and he needed a new career. Through working at the high school, he found he liked teaching students, especially struggling learners, so he went back to school for a teaching certificate. After two years, he was finishing his last class and would student teach in the fall.

When I walked in the house, the kids were dressed in their bathing suits, sitting at the kitchen stools eating Life cereal. I rinsed the freshly picked strawberries and laid them on a dish towel on the island. I was in the garden much longer than I thought. We would have to use the sunscreen spray today.

"Come here, Zach. I need to spray your back. Natalie, use the sun screen stick on your face and then give it to Ryan."

Zach and I walked out on the porch. "Hold out your arms and close your eyes," I told him.

He took a deep breath and held it. Turning him around, a cloud of sun screen fell on every exposed area, covering him from his neck to his toes. The kids were familiar with our morning routine, but I had to move them along. They were groggy from staying up late.

"Get your goggles and towels and meet me in the car. We are the drop off for car pool today."

Everyone scrambled into the van, and as they buckled in, I closed the sliding door.

After swim practice, we ate a quick lunch and headed back to the pool. In the afternoon, when the pool officially opened, we were usually one of the first cars in the parking lot. The boys unbuckled their seatbelts before I put the car in park.

"Should we go to our spot?" Ryan asked, already holding his towel, a ball, and the cooler.

"Our spot" changed each year, depending on the ages of our kids. The first few years, we sat close to the baby pool and a covered porch. As the children became more independent, we moved around the pool. We were finally in the older kid area next to a huge water slide. They hurried past the front desk, dropped chairs, towels, coolers, and their flip-flops in a heap on the grass. The boys took off for the diving boards, and Natalie wandered off to look for some friends.

There were many years when taking the kids to the pool was a lot of work, chasing them around, moving from the baby pool to the big pool and back again, worrying about changing their swimmy diapers, and getting them home before they had a meltdown at nap time. We were past that phase now.

Once I got everyone to the pool, I plopped into a beach chair. My work was done. The moms, along with an occasional dad, could sit and talk, uninterrupted, at least until the whistle blew. On the hour, the life guards blew their long whistle, signaling a fifteen-minute adult swim.

The kids came running back to our fortress of towels, umbrellas, and chairs.

"Can we have money for the concession stand?" groups of kids started asking their moms.

The first adult swim, one of the grown-ups would answer, "You just ate lunch. Go play." The kids would run off to the large field, choosing teams for a quick game of whiffle ball. A few minutes later, the whistle sounded again, and they were all back in the pool.

I pulled out my magazine and started flipping through it. I loved to try new recipes that used ingredients from my garden. I dog-eared a page for basil butter to use with corn on the cob. In the summer, I always had more energy to cook. After a few minutes, I remembered the latest selection from my book club was in my bag. We called ours "The Lazy Girl Book Club." Some book clubs are serious, reading and thoughtfully critiquing a book every month. In contrast, mine met once every three–six months, and it was common that the majority of ladies hadn't read the book. The club consisted of a group of friends taking turns choosing a book and then hosting a discussion session with food and drinks. Mostly, it was just a good excuse to get together. I opened the book and started reading. It was a light read, perfect for the pool.

About ten pages into the book, the whistles sounded again and our blankets were immediately overtaken by kids. An hour went by so quickly. *Why couldn't sixty minutes pass this fast when I was in the classroom?*

By 4:00, when the life guards blew their final whistles, only a handful of people remained at the club. The kids were tired from being in the sun and swimming all day.

"It's time to go. Make sure you each have your flip-flops and towel," I said.

On the way home, we stopped at the local orchard early in the summer to buy blueberries, and later in the season, we would stop for watermelon.

As the kids hung up their towels in the house, I gathered some lettuce leaves, spring onions, and peas from our garden to make a salad. It would be a nice night to eat dinner outside.

As the kids cleared the table after dinner, I walked into the garden to pick some fresh mint. I had planted it for the sole purpose of making mojitos in the summer. I muddled the mint, squeezed the lime, and poured in some Rum and Sprite. Scott was sitting on the porch swing his parents had bought us as a wedding gift, listening to Jack Johnson. I relaxed into my side of the soft rope seat and the comfortable back and forth motion. We sat swinging, listening to the pack of kids running around our yard, hiding in the playhouse, and playing Zombie tag for hours.

Each day in the summer seemed almost identical to the one before. Weeks quickly passed by, and before I knew it, it was the end of July.

As we were in the kitchen one evening, Scott asked, "Do we have any plans next weekend? I was thinking we could go listen to music at the vineyard."

I walked over to look at the calendar clipped to the side of the refrigerator. I couldn't remember anything, but I hadn't looked at it in days. Flipping the page to the next month to see Saturday, a panicked feeling hit me instantly as I realized that in a few days, it would be August. My stomach dropped at the thought of returning to school. The whole summer I pushed thoughts of school to the back of my mind, hoping we would win the lottery or have some other stroke of good fortune, and I wouldn't have to go back. Realistically, it was almost impossible. I hardly ever even bought a scratch off ticket.

I groaned. "We have a swim meet on Saturday, but the rest of the weekend is free."

"What's wrong?" he asked.

"Summer is almost over." I pouted.

Scott knew that "back to school time" was a sensitive issue for me, one he avoided as much as possible.

"You still have a month of vacation. Most people don't get a month *total*, and you still have a month *left*," he reminded me.

We had the same conversation every year at this time. I tried to focus on the positive aspects of my career and having summers off was the biggest benefit of teaching.

I remember a Double Bubble gum wrapper with a cartoon printed on it. A kid asked a teacher, *"What are the three best reasons to be a teacher?"* The teacher, sitting at her desk responded, *"June, July, and August."*

I knew how rare it was that I could spend three months with my kids, but there were so many other special times I had to miss. I was filled with regret not only about the summer ending but also for all the times I had not been there over the years, beginning when they were babies and still needed their mom. I went back to teach before they could walk, missing out on their daily activities. I never got to watch my children get on the bus their first day of school or be there when they read poetry during classroom programs or pick them up from school when they were sick. Every August, at least one time before the school year started, I would end up crying.

They were getting older and needed me less and less. The time would come soon when they wouldn't need me at all.

All the things I had planned to do with the kids over the summer crept into my head. We should have gone to a museum or maybe made a trip to Washington, D.C. *How did the summer go by so quickly*? I felt like a terrible mom. Maybe we could squeeze in something fun in the next few weeks. I had to make the most of the time we had left. I knew we wouldn't do any of those things once school started. For a few more weeks, I could push the dread of school back down.

All the practices for fall sports began in early August. Scott's football team had two to three practices a day. Natalie had two practices daily for tennis, and the boys were playing little league football and had one long practice each night.

For years, I had gathered all their sports gear, filled their water bottles, and drove them to practices. Now, they were old enough to get ready themselves, and coaches didn't require parents on the sidelines. I suddenly found myself with free time—hours and hours of free time. I had mixed feelings about my new freedom. As much as I had craved a moment to myself when the kids were younger and calling, "Mom, Mom, Mom," when I tried to do anything alone, I now felt nervous entering this new stage in my life. *What was I going to do?* I did what I usually do when I have nervous energy to burn. I cleaned and organized the house. I tried to get myself prepared for the hectic pace of the school year.

I spent days washing the windows, cleaning out the refrigerator, and going through the kids' closets. I never had this much time to myself, and I quickly ran out of things to do. I started to feel down. I was accustomed to feeling depressed as the school year neared, but this year seemed worse for some reason. I was thinking about my wedding anniversary on August 12th and how I would be spending it alone because Scott would be at football practices. I decided to call my best friend, Janie, to invite her over for lunch.

*"Hey, girl, hey,"* Janie answered.

*"Heeeyyy, girl, heeeyy!"*

We both broke out laughing. Since we met in 2nd grade, we spent equal amounts of time being silly and talking.

"Do you want to come over for a long lunch tomorrow?"

I was happy when she immediately accepted. Spending time with her always put me in a better mood.

"Is everything OK? You sound a little down." She knew me better than anyone else. I couldn't hide my feelings from her.

"Yeah, just in a funk about school starting."

I was familiar with the funk. It was something I went through every year and not just at back-to-school time. I had even devised different plans to keep my spirits up and make it through each school year because, at the end of the school day, I came home feeling angry.

One year, I decided to reward myself with a café mocha. Each Friday, I lined up at the drive thru to treat myself to the hot drink for completing another week.

Another year, I tried to focus on my nutrition. I did weekly meal planning, finding healthy recipes from my vegan friend's cookbook to make for dinner and bring to school for lunch. We ate a lot of quinoa, avocados, and kale. I laughed when my students asked, *"What is that terrible smell?"* I pretended I had no idea where the strong odor was coming from, but I knew for sure it came from the kale cooking in a roaster in Leslie's room. I could only imagine the faces her kids were making being so close to the smell.

I tried riding my bike to and from school. It was a hilly six mile ride each way. There was a lot of preparation and organization needed to transport myself, a change of clothing, make up, lunch, and books for the day. All the planning was worth the freedom I felt at the end of each day when I hopped on my bike and took off. It was the feeling I had as a kid riding around my neighborhood. Using my muscles helped me decompress, and by the time I made it home, I was a little tired and in a pretty good mood. I would have ridden my bike to school every day, but rain, ice, and freezing temperatures kept me off the roads for several months.

I used exercise to help reduce the frustration. For a few years, I ran, almost daily, when I came home. I didn't run a certain number of minutes or miles, I ran until I didn't feel angry anymore. Sometimes, by the time I was done, the bottoms of my feel ached from pounding them so hard on the road. I couldn't keep running like I was, so I had tried to do yoga and lift weights, searching for the perfect cure for my mood. Exercise had worked in the past, so Janie suggested we figure out how to fit exercise into my fall schedule. With all the activities going on in my family, my workouts seemed to be at the bottom of the list.

I was eager to see what she could come up with because nothing seemed to be working the last few years to relieve stress.

It was hot the day Janie came over. I had made iced tea and picked some zucchini, tomatoes, and basil to make us lunch. She sat on a stool in the kitchen, and we talked while I fried the zucchini. I alternated slices of zucchini, tomatoes, and fresh mozzarella to make little stacks and then drizzled balsamic vinegar and olive oil on top.

"What's going on? You don't seem your happy self," Janie said.

"I have been feeling sad and even crying for the last few weeks. I don't know what's wrong," I confessed.

When we finished eating, she told me to get some paper, and we could go out on the back porch to figure out my new exercise plan. I grabbed a spiral bound notebook that was lying on my kitchen desk and went outside to the wrought iron table. I was ready to work on an exercise plan when Janie asked me a question I wasn't expecting.

"Do you really not know why you're feeling sad?"

Confused, I said, "No, I really don't."

Janie suddenly became serious and said, "Do you want me to tell you why?" She's one of the most honest people I know and wants to make sure you are asking for her advice before giving it. It was the first time, since my kids were babies and I had to return to school, that I felt this sad. I had always thought once they were in school and didn't need me at home that teaching would be easier. So why was I so upset?

She said matter-of-factly, "You're done with teaching. You don't want to do it anymore."

I was shocked. Going back to school was something I disliked every year, but that wasn't anything new. It couldn't be that. I remember the rest of our conversation like it happened in slow motion.

Janie said, "I came here today to help you with an exercise plan, but that's not what you really need. You want to quit your job, so we're going to talk about that."

I stopped breathing. I was terrified. Janie wrote the date August 12th on the top of the new notebook page and the words "Quit Your Job Now" and then drew a box around it. Then she looked up at me and realized I was in panic mode. She added the word "gracefully" beside "Quit Your Job Now."

---

## *Quitting Gracefully*

- *Allow yourself time to create a plan.*
- *Give plenty of notice so that others can adapt to your vacancy.*
- *Although it didn't work out, be grateful for the opportunity you were given.*
- *Be honest about your intentions to move on.*
- *Reserve all negative comments. Be remembered in a positive light.*

*Whether it's a job, relationship, or volunteer position, life is too short to spend your time doing something you don't love.*

*Is there something you need to quit gracefully in your life?*

---

# CHAPTER THREE

# *Assess the Situation*

It all begins with a plan. Make a plan to get started.

Right away, while Janie sat on the back porch relaxed, I started coming up with reasons why I couldn't quit my job now. There were only two weeks left until school started; it would be unprofessional to quit this late. My classroom was mostly set up. I had sent postcards to my students to introduce myself as their teacher and invite them to meet me for an open house next week. It would be inconvenient for the district to have to interview for a new teacher this close to the beginning of the school year.

And then there was Scott. He wouldn't want me to quit. In a few weeks, he would be starting a challenging student teaching semester. I remember the tough schedule: teaching school all day and writing plans in the evenings and weekends. I had been grateful to live at home with my parents that semester. Having my mom cook dinner and do my laundry allowed me to devote all my time to preparing lessons.

In addition to a rigorous student teaching schedule, Scott was going to continue to coach football. To student teach, he had to give up his classroom aide position. It didn't pay much, but we would be missing his income for four months. I wasn't as worried about cutting expenses during student teaching because he would finish in December. It was rare to have open positions in the middle of the year. Realistically, summer would be the earliest he could get a teaching job.

*How would we afford our house?* As much as I wanted to change, I was gripped by fear. I didn't want to teach, but there was comfort in familiarity. Janie started brainstorming a list of questions I needed to answer to figure out how Scott and I could financially manage this change:

"How much does it cost you to live in this house?"

"How much do you need to make each month?"

"Are there ways you could finance this change?"

With each question, I just sat there, stunned into silence and scared at the possibilities she presented. The fear in my stomach was like being at the top of a roller coaster, looking at the deep drop below. It was too much too soon for me. She went to the top of the next page notebook page and wrote, "Quitting Your Job in One Year."

She passed the notebook to me. "If quitting now doesn't seem like an option, write down steps you could take toward quitting that would feel more comfortable."

I thought about what I could do and wrote, "Save money this year, downsize, and move into town where we could walk to everything." I was ready for our talk to be over, but Janie moved on to another crucial question.

"What job would you like to do?"

Thinking about a new career was a lot less scary than figuring out how I would finance a whole life change. I came up with a few options: realtor, life coach, and registered dietician.

The last thing Janie did before she left was write in her curly handwriting, *"I Am Quitting My Job,"* large enough to cover a whole notebook page.

After Janie left, I closed the notebook and put in on the kitchen desk. As much as I wanted to leave my job, I felt in my heart that the work we had done that day would not change my circumstances at all. I went into the front yard to cut the dead flowers off our rose bushes and went on with the rest of my day.

I had always found it easy to fall asleep. Typically, within a few minutes of my head hitting the pillow, I was already dreaming. I was such a deep sleeper that Scott didn't let me have the alarm clock on my side of the bed because I had been known to shut it off and not even remember hearing it. The day Janie had come over for lunch, I fell asleep quickly that night, like usual.

Completely out of the ordinary, I woke up at 2:00 am. I was suddenly wide awake, the conversation with Janie replaying in my mind. I lay awake for two hours, contemplating how I was going to resign from my position. I made a decision, in the morning I would start figuring out how much money we needed each month for our bills and think about what I would do for a job if I actually quit teaching.

I don't remember when I became a list maker, but I recall making them as a teenager. There

41

had been a few times in high school when I didn't write down a homework assignment and then recalled it in the middle of the night or as I walked into the class the next day. Writing things down decreased my anxiety about forgetting something. Making a list helped me gather my thoughts and plan out what I needed to do. I felt a great sense of accomplishment crossing off things I had completed.

During my first year of teaching, lists were a crucial part of my days. Scott and I got engaged three months into the school year and started to build a house almost immediately. I had to remember supplies to bring to school for my lessons, wedding details that needed attention, and projects that needed completing at our new home. The daily lists I kept in a hardbound floral Victoria's Secret planner helped keep everything clear in my mind. I still have a few planners I kept as memories of that time. It is amazing to see how much energy I had.

Despite having been awake for several hours the night before, I woke up early the next morning, full of energy. I gathered all our regular monthly bills and the notebook Janie and I had written in. Scott and I were cautious with money and didn't have much debt, but it was important to figure out our income and expenses.

During our marriage, I had taken three unpaid maternity leaves, each one lasting from six months to over a year. We learned how to cut expenses where we could. I remember eating a lot of pasta and using all the vegetables I could from our first garden to cut our grocery bills. Scott and I even started using hair clippers to do his haircuts at home. He cut the front and top, and I did the back. Although a man's haircut didn't cost very much, everything added up and it was one less expense.

Later, when the boys were young, I taught half-day kindergarten for a few years. I left the house at 8:00 am and was home right after lunch. If I had to leave the kids, it was the perfect amount of time, but half-day had a draw back—it also meant half-pay. When Scott's home building business started slowing down, I had to go back to a full-time teaching position.

Now, I was considering leaving my job at a time when he wouldn't have any income and we had the additional expenses of his college tuition and books. Because we had needed to be so careful with our money for the last several years, there wasn't a whole lot of excess left to trim from the budget. *How could we possibly do this?*

Then I thought about our home. I carefully chose every fixture, floor covering, and paint color in the house. *How could we leave this house?* It was in a great neighborhood, with so many kids within walking distance. The boys always had a friend close by. If I could figure out a career where I earned the same salary as teaching, then we wouldn't have to move. My goal was to leave teaching. I didn't need to disrupt my whole family in the process.

The summer was quickly coming to an end, and fall sports practices were underway. I was alone in the house with our cat, Piper.

With no one needing my attention, it was a good time to refocus on my health. I decided to try a three-day cleanse plan. I talked my sister, Les, into joining me. We went to the store and bought beets, celery, ginger, apples, carrots, and bags full of produce to make breakfast and lunch smoothies for three days. It took a lot of prep work to clean and cut everything. When we finished, I had mounds of peelings to throw in my composter. Large containers full of the concoctions went in the refrigerator.

Day 1 of the cleanse: I drank the morning juice. It wasn't horrible, but it wasn't what I would have called a "smoothie." My stomach growled during the morning, missing my usual bowl of cereal. I found myself watching the clock, eager for the time when I could drink my lunch portion. I realized that since all my meals were premade, I didn't need to go to the grocery store, plan any meals, or prep or cook anything, and there was no cleanup. I didn't expect how much free time the cleanse would afford me. I had even more time to think and consider my big change.

I got out my notebook and turned to a new page where I began a list of potential careers. I started with the ones I had talked about with Janie. In total, I came up with thirteen ideas that interested me. I also listed temporary jobs I could do to make money. Toying with the idea of completely changing my life was exciting and unsettling, and I had to take a break.

To clear my mind, I started organizing the large sideboard in our dining room. There were a ton of drawers and storage that we hardly used, so it was a good place to start.

As I evaluated the napkin rings and tablecloths, I daydreamed about the different careers. I had never given much thought to what I wanted as a career when I was in high school. I considered how much I liked to cook and grow herbs and food in my own garden. Maybe Scott and I could open a restaurant. I fantasized about opening a small café, creating an interesting, industrial, repurposed space where people could meet for coffee, healthy foods, and pastries. I only wanted to be open for breakfast and lunch. We had discussed the idea of opening a restaurant before, and I knew Scott would prefer to serve dinner and have a bar that stayed open until 2:00 am. Even if we could come together on the type of food we would serve and the hours of operation, it would be a huge financial commitment and a gamble for both of us to be involved with a restaurant. It wouldn't allow us much time with our family and friends. I tried on other careers in my mind, like a wedding planner, restaurant food critic, and professional organizer. I liked remaining open to any possibility.

I was surprised at the amount of energy I had during the cleanse. I was physically active during the day and took long walks each evening while the kids were at practices. By nighttime, my body was exhausted and I fell asleep quickly. After a few hours, I woke up. It was like my brain was trying to tell me, *"You had enough rest. Get up. You have important work to do here."* For hours, I would be alert and clear, thinking about my life.

Each night, my feelings became more intense, and on the third night, I went down to the kitchen and started to write. The words were flowing out of me faster than my hand could write them. I truly felt like my inner voice was speaking to me through the pen, giving me reasons why I deserved to make the change. This voice was strong and confident in my decision to leave and made me feel it was possible.

At first when I was writing, I was inspired and excited that my life was heading in a new direction. The excitement was short lived though, as I started crying, engulfed by a feeling of sadness. The story of my life—the only story I had ever imagined—was now changing. Even though I wanted desperately to leave my job, it was all I had known as an adult. It had been my path since high school, and more than that, being a teacher was my identity. *Now who would I be?*

To quit teaching meant a lot of uncertainty. *Where would we live?* Would we be able to afford to stay in our house? I worried about letting down Scott and our kids. We would have to leave all our friends in the neighborhood. Our whole lives would change because of me. I felt so selfish. *Why should their lives have to change because of me? What if it was the wrong decision?* This fear had paralyzed me into staying in my job for so many years.

I wanted to resign when Natalie was a newborn. I desperately longed to be home with her, rocking her, taking her for walks in the stroller, and being there for her. I wanted to give her the best life. But an opportunity came to build a house in a better school district, so I reluctantly went back to teaching at the end of my maternity leave.

Deep in my soul, I knew I wanted to leave my job, but it wasn't clear to me how to claim the next step of my life. I had waited years for the magic moment when the circumstances were right; when it worked for everyone else, until after we had the next child, when Scott's business was more secure, and finally when we were making "more money." I was beginning to realize there would never be a perfect time.

*What would my parents, who spent their entire careers in education, think of my decision?* They knew how I felt. Although they didn't understand, they knew from the second year of teaching that I wanted to leave.

I fought with my inner self, pleading for a safer way. Maybe I could make it to retirement. I was halfway there. I could start another career then. I felt the sensible, practical side of me taking over.

Then I thought about my grandmother, Nora. I had been close with her, staying with her for weeks in the summer. She had a massive heart attack at the age of fifty and died before she turned sixty. *What if I spent my whole life at a job I didn't feel was right for me, putting everything on hold, and died after I retired?* I heard stories of this exact scenario. *What if I didn't even make it to retirement? Would it matter to my family that I had stuck it out for financial reasons? Would I have made the best use of my life?* There are no guarantees how long we are on this Earth. I had to use the rest of my days doing something that brought me joy. I couldn't wait fifteen more years to live my life. I needed to live it now. My health and happiness where important, and it was up to me to fight for it. The years of my life were going by quickly, and I needed to stand up for what I wanted. I was the one holding myself back.

> **"If your dreams do not scare you, they are not big enough."**
>
> - Ellen Johnson Sirleaf
>
> - *Are you holding yourself back?*
>
> - *What is the biggest dream you have for yourself?*

# CHAPTER FOUR

# *Imagine What You Want*

Think about what it is you really want. Don't be
clouded by other's ideas.

I stood at the glass door and watched the long line of children walk across the school yard. It was my turn to let the students into the building after lunch recess. I would rather not be the first point of contact after recess though because it turned me into the enforcer of rules. I heard reports from classmates about every child who didn't stay in line or didn't let someone join their game.

I held the door as the line of first graders filed past me into their classrooms. A blond-haired girl in my class ran toward me with a concerned look on her face. I could see something had been spilled on her shirt, and it looked like chocolate milk.

"Mrs. Souders, a boy at recess yelled the 'S' word at me." As her classmates took their coats off in the hallway and hung them in their lockers, the area around the girl and I turned into a rubbernecking scene. They craned their necks to hear what the girl was saying.

"Go into the room and get a partner to practice your math fact cards." I said to the class. I would have to talk with the girl in the hallway to find out more information. It turned out the boy's name was Tyler or maybe Skyler, the girl was not sure, but he was not in our classroom. Now, I had the task of locating Tyler or Skyler and questioning him.

I walked into Leslie's room to see if she had a student by either name—she did. I asked him to come into the hallway. I hoped he was the person I was looking for so that my search would be over. The boy's hair was matted and sweaty from recess, and he looked terrified. The girl was waiting in the hall by the lockers and was quick to identify the boy as the offender. I asked her to repeat what she told me happened at recess. She began to tell the story about how they were playing tag around the tanbark area and then he yelled the "S" word. The boy stared at me, not saying anything.

Then looking at the ground, he said, "I did not say the bad 'S' word." It was never easy to get the true story out of two six-year-old children.

I looked back at the girl and ask her to tell us what "S" word the boy said. She didn't want to say it. She was afraid she would get in trouble.

I told her, "It's OK to say it to me. We need to know the word."

She quietly said, "Shut up."

I quickly explained, "It's not nice to say, 'Shut up,' but it is not the bad 'S' word."

I dismissed the boy and hurried back into the classroom, hoping that everyone was in their seats without problems.

Outside of school, I would have been able to laugh at the mix up, but my students rarely saw that side of me. I was rigid with my schedule and annoyed when it was thrown off. I would have to rush through the math lesson and probably wouldn't have enough time to adequately explain the practice game I planned to play. I felt guilty I didn't have more patience with those situations.

When the students left for their special class that afternoon, I pulled out my notebook of ideas and lists again. I had started bringing it with me to school each day. I had several beautiful bound notebooks, each one with less than five pages written, but now, I had a lot to write.

One of the biggest decisions I had to make was choosing my next career. When Janie had been helping me on the porch, I struggled identifying what I wanted in a job. The only things I could come up with were that I wanted to be able to drive during the day and wear jeans and sneakers. She encouraged me to write a list of things I *didn't* want in my next career.

> 1. To wear nylons (wearing nylons is like "nails on a chalkboard" for me. They made my skin crawl.)
> 2. To dress up every day (see Number 1)
> 3. Trapped in an office or cubical
> 4. A 9–5, inflexible schedule

My list of dislikes wasn't long, but it was a start.

If I was going to uncover what I wanted, I had to start slowing down. My classroom aide, Nancy, was a brilliant and observant person. I loved talking with her every morning before the students rushed in and the day started. Some days, I would need a second cup of tea, and she figured out that my throat always got scratchy at a certain time of the month. I joked that she knew my body better than I did, but it was true. I was so busy with day to day life that I didn't listen to myself. It was important that I allowed my mind to wander and explore the possibilities. I decided to turn off the radio when I was in the car and spend more time being quiet.

A quote I heard from Sarah Ban Breathnach on Super Soul Sunday really hit home. She said, *"Most people are too busy living the life they planned to live the life they want."* That was me. I had taken the path to become a teacher when I was eighteen years old because I needed to choose a college major. I hadn't been drawn to teaching, it just seemed easy and like a natural decision for me to follow in my parents' footsteps. Now, I was just following along with this story I had started.

I read a book about journaling dreams that explained how you can use it as a tool to tap into your unconscious mind. I decided to try it. I kept an open notebook and pen on my nightstand. Each morning, before opening my eyes or putting a foot on the floor, I wrote down the dreams, thoughts, and feelings I was having at that very moment. Then I would get out of bed and go to the bathroom. When I came back, I would read what I had written and try to fill in any information that came to mind. I was amazed at how quickly the dreams left me. It was entertaining to read them later and try to remember more of the dream. I had been journaling my dreams for a while when I decided to reread and analyze them. Some made no sense at all while others had a clear connection to what was going on in my waking life. I noticed I had a nightmare that repeated itself often: I was in a speeding car, driving along a cliffside road. I imagined it would be somewhere along the coast of California. The car was out of control, going faster and faster and moving dangerously close to the edge. In the dream, I was trying to drive the car from the backseat without being able to see the road. I realized this nightmare was a metaphor for my life. My life was barreling ahead full speed, out of control, and I had no idea where I was going. I needed to get my eyes on the road and take control of the wheel. I needed to be the driver of my own car.

Occasionally, there were dreams or messages that seemed to be on a loop. One particular night, the image was a triangle with the pointed side facing down, and the message that kept repeating was "*You have to know where you've been to know where you are going.*" It was a powerful, clear message to me. I had to analyze what I had been doing and how I got to this point in my life if I wanted to move forward in a different direction. I was amazed that I was receiving instructions through my dreams to evaluate my life and take control.

I had read about the law of attraction and understood the concept of first imagining what you wanted to create. I tried to imagine what my new life would look like. I decided to create a vision board. I went into the dining room with glue, scissors, poster board, and a stack of old *Martha Stewart*, *Oprah*, and *Whole Living* magazines. I quickly tore out pictures, quotes, phrases, or colors I liked. When I was done, I had a stack of pages on the table.

After I trimmed neatly around each one, I started arranging and gluing them to the poster board. Before my eyes, the life I wanted revealed itself. Words and phrases jumped out at me: A NEW TWIST ON FAMILY TIME, CREATE, and NEW USES FOR OLD THINGS. I was envisioning a life where I could use creativity and follow my passion. In the center, I chose to glue a quote by Steve Jobs:

*"The only way to do great work is to love what you do. If you haven't found it yet, keep looking. Don't settle. As with all matters of the heart, you'll know it when you find it."*

I was excited by the revelations on the vision board and the dreams I was having at night. I was planning a huge life change and uncovering important aspects of myself that I wanted to share with Scott, but I had to keep it to myself—it wasn't a good time.

Scott just started his student teaching semester, the final step before he would be a certified teacher. I knew he was nervous moving into a completely new role at this stage in his life, and as he was getting ready to enter the profession, I wanted to leave. *Would it make him question his choice?* Scott certainly didn't need the added stress of selling our house to his already full plate. I would hold on to the secret until he was finished in December. When I was excited about my career change or having severe doubts about my plan, I called Les or Janie. A few times, Scott had come home when I was on the phone with one of them, and I quickly changed the conversation. I was uncharacteristically quiet around him, but it was the only way I could keep from letting something slip.

One night, a few weeks after I started thinking about quitting my job, Scott walked into our bedroom. He was still dressed in the athletic shorts and t-shirt from practice, his football whistle hung around his neck.

He looked at me sitting in a chair, writing in my journal. "What's going on with you?"

I still remember the first time I saw him in junior high school. I immediately noticed his dark, thick hair and eyes as he stepped onto the school bus.

I whispered to my friend Jen, "Who is *that*?" We had been friends since I was four years old. She was a grade older and always seemed wiser, so I turned to her for all my questions about boys.

"That's Scott Souders. He's in my grade."

Our bus ride was an hour long, rural route, which gave me a lot of time to watch him. I noticed that he stood up for weaker kids, telling bullies to leave them alone. I saw his huge smile and friendly laugh. I was never so excited to ride the bus to school. I hardly missed a day. I wanted to get to know him, so I casually chose seats close to him. We talked and flirted with each other for a few years. When we were in high school, he asked me to wear his football jersey, our school symbol that meant I was his girlfriend. Now as we talked in our bedroom, we had been together through high school, college, and over seventeen years of marriage. I didn't want to lie to him. We were a team.

I blurted out, "I decided I'm only teaching one more year. We have one year to figure out how to make it work." It was nothing new for me to say I wanted to quit. But this time I was stating it instead of complaining.

Scott stared at me. He didn't say a word.

## *Finding your passion and purpose*

- *What would you do even if no one paid you?*
- *What comes naturally to you? What do your friends say you are good at?*
- *What can you be working on and time seems to fly by?*

### *How to Make Your Own Vision Board*

1. *Get a stack of various old magazines.*
2. *Quickly—without analyzing—rip out any pictures, quotes, or colors that catch your eye.*
3. *Once you have a pile of torn out pieces, trim them up nicely.*
4. *Lay out all the pictures. What do you notice? Do some things repeat?*
5. *Arrange them and glue them on poster board. Add any words or phrases you would like to make your vision board complete.*

# PURGE

The purging part of the organizing process scares many people. They imagine someone tearing through their prized possessions, telling them what they do or do not need to keep. In reality, you are the only one who can decide what's important.

I have a different, more positive view of purging. I see it as a process of shedding the things that are no longer you to reveal the truest you underneath. Maybe you have grown and changed, and the items no longer fit with who you are or who you are becoming. You may have acquired things that you never really wanted. Either way, there is no need to feel guilty about change. It happens to everyone. Getting rid of these things that are weighing you down is a healthy process.

Think of it like pruning a tree, it actually makes the tree grow stronger. It is freeing to finally get down to the real you.

CHAPTER FIVE

# *Consider What's Important*

Decide what's essential and make that your main focus.

Teaching drained me. From the moment the students burst into the room, I felt like I was running a three-ring circus. I answered an email from a parent as I watched a child use blocks to demonstrate their addition skills. While I listened to a group of children read, I had to use "the look" to keep the rest of the class quiet—juggling to keep all the balls in the air and meet everyone's needs. What depleted my energy the most though was putting on the mask of being a teacher. The weight of pretending that teaching was my passion was exhausting. If you looked around and watched me teach you wouldn't notice anything wrong, but I had the vision that if someone could "unzip" me and peer inside, they would be shocked to see it was completely empty.

When I left school at the end of the day, I longed to go home and do something for myself, by myself. I wanted time alone to recharge my battery with no one calling my name.

As I walked in the door with my lunch bag, school bag, and purse still in hand, I used my feet to kick my kids' shoes and backpacks out of my path. They got home before I did and dropped their things as they walked in the door. *This wouldn't happen if I was here when they got home.*

Set off by the clutter, I immediately started barking orders. "Move your backpacks. Take your shoes to your room."

I scrambled to figure out what to have for dinner. As the left overs reheated in the microwave, I looked through school papers, asked about homework, and opened the mail. We ate quickly and left the dishes in the sink. As the kids piled into the minivan, I was aware that the rest of the night I would be driving, transporting kids back and forth from practices.

While I drove, I listened to my kids talking with their friends. *Did I even say hello when I came home or ask anyone about their day?* I started creating a mental to do list: write out bills, get a gift for my niece's birthday party, find an orange shirt for Ryan to wear for orange day tomorrow... The van door slid open and kids piled in and out.

A few hours later, I pulled into the garage, home for the night. Time to do some of the things on my list that had gotten longer as the night went on. I walked in the kitchen to see Natalie looking in the pantry.

"Mom, I just remembered I signed up to bring cookies to French class tomorrow. I looked in the pantry, and we don't have any."

I spent the last three hours in the car. I was not about to go to the store now. *She should have told me earlier.* It was after 8:00 pm, I already had a sink full of dishes, and now I would have to make cookies. I felt guilty for being so angry and frustrated. Baking was one of my favorite things to do, but I just couldn't enjoy it knowing I had to go to school in the morning. I still hadn't had any time to myself.

It bothered me that during the school year, I had a short temper. I needed time alone to refuel. I had to reclaim time for me. I decided to take back Sundays and use that one day of the week to do all the things that made me happy. I started with a cup of coffee, squirt of chocolate syrup, and some coconut creamer and then settled into the corner spot in the couch I called my nest. With my heavy blanket, nicknamed "Cover O' Sleep," on me, I watched the *Saturday Night Live* episode that recorded the night before along with the latest episodes of *Portlandia* and *Super Store*.

Next, I would get out the notebook Janie and I wrote in to take notes as I watched Oprah's *SuperSoul Sunday*. Each week, she invited a guest to talk about the big issues in life. I jotted down quotes that inspired me. When they discussed finding your passion or purpose in life, it resonated with me so deeply that I welled up with tears. I remember one guest talked about making a list of what was important to you and comparing it to how you actually spent your time and energy. It seemed like a simple exercise, so I wrote down my list of important things.

1. Making memories with my family
2. Spending time with friends
3. My health

Next, I wrote down where I spent my time and energy. Number one was at my job. I don't think it's unusual to spend a lot of time and energy on your career. But my career was not on my list of important things. I was putting the majority of time and energy into something that didn't bring me joy, and I continued to do it year after year so that we could afford our house. But as I sat on my couch, it struck me that *having a big house was not on my list of important items either*. A lot of people want to live in a big house, but that was never my goal. If we sold our house, I could quit my job and spend more quality time with my family.

My health was third on my list of important things. Over the past few years, I had suffered from ovarian cysts. The first time I had one, my sister and I were training for a mini-triathlon we were going to do with our brother, Chad. For three months, we ran, rode our bikes, and swam laps at an indoor pool.

One week before the event, driving home from getting a haircut, I felt a sharp, stabbing pain. It was so intense, like nothing I had felt before, that I could barely speak. I knew something serious was wrong, and without an appointment I went directly to my doctor's office. He quickly sent me to the hospital where they discovered an ovarian cyst had ruptured. I had surgery and couldn't compete in the triathlon. It took me a few weeks to recover physically, and I was really disappointed that I missed the triathlon.

Following the initial episode, painful cysts started developing about every seven months. My longtime friend, Kristin, a registered nurse and therapeutic chef in California, recommended I see an acupuncturist. I didn't know what to expect from our appointment, so when I booked my first session with Becky, I told her it was for general health.

In our initial session, she asked, "Do you work? Tell me about your job?"

"I am a teacher. I've taught in different schools and grade levels but mostly elementary," I told her.

Kindly, she said, "I'm sorry you don't like your job."

I was stunned by her response. "I didn't say I didn't like my job."

"You didn't have to. Your body language did. You crossed your legs and squeezed your arms around your waist like you were holding yourself in tight."

I had wanted to quit my job and talked about it every year, but I had never truly acknowledged that

I didn't like it. She could see I was squeezing myself into being a teacher, and it didn't fit me.

Becky wasn't the only medical professional to notice the effect my job had on my health. Early in my teaching career, I was diagnosed with high blood pressure and prescribed medication to control it. My physicians were surprised when my blood pressure routinely dropped in the summer and when I was home on maternity leaves. During the school year, I experienced frequent migraines and neck problems. My chiropractor commented a few times, "You barely need adjusting over the summer." If I really valued my health like I claimed, then I needed to make a change in my career.

A few months had passed since the night I told Scott I was going to quit teaching. At first, he had been shocked and a little angry with me for "springing this on him," but within a few weeks of our brief conversation, he started looking on the internet for potential homes. Any chance we had, we swiped through pictures of homes, imagining our lives in different towns. All of the houses we looked at were either too expensive or would cost too much to fix. *What if we didn't find a house that was cheap enough? Would I have to keep teaching?* We hadn't put our house up for sale or said much to the kids yet since we hadn't found anything that suited our price range.

One day in March, when the boys typically had baseball and lacrosse practices, all sports were cancelled because of rain. Scott and I decided to use a Christmas gift card for a rare weeknight date. It wasn't that I loved the Olive Garden, but we had been trying to save money and hadn't eaten out in a while. It was a treat to be going out for dinner.

After we ordered, Scott nervously chewed his nails and looked around the restaurant when he said, "I'm really worried about you quitting your job and selling our house."

"I know."

"The market's down. It isn't a good time to sell," he said.

"Yeah."

He continued, "I built our house, and since our business closed, it was probably the last one I will ever build."

I sat there, thinking about our home. How our children had grown up in that house, about the hill in our backyard where we built a playset, and how all the neighbors came to sled when it snowed. I had chosen every paint color and fixture. *We really liked our house.*

He was worried, and I was too. We never made risky decisions. Financially, our whole plan hinged on the possibility that we could sell our house and find a less expensive one. We had been looking for months and hadn't found any that would save us money.

He was also concerned about not getting a teaching position, and neither of us would have job security or benefits if I quit my job. "By going through with this plan, I think we're committing financial suicide," he added.

Immediately, I felt so much pressure. It wasn't too late. I could call it all off right then. I hadn't made anything official yet. I still had my job. No one knew at school, except my closest friends who were sworn to secrecy. My stomach hurt.

"I need to go to the bathroom."

I hurried to be alone in the dimly lit room. I needed to clear my mind. It would be so easy to stop and give in now, but I had given up what I wanted so many times in the past for the good of the family. I kept pushing through teaching year after year. I had encouraged and supported Scott through career changes, urging him to do whatever made him happy.

*Even though his homebuilding business closed, didn't he still have the skills to build another house later if we wanted to?* We had built three houses already. Was it even that important to build again? I realized that if I gave in now, I would be giving up my happiness for the sake of having a house we had built with our own hands. We had lived in a big, beautiful, new house the last seven years. Our house wasn't worth the price tag of working at a job that made me unhappy.

I had finally figured out I could no longer be happy teaching. I was at a pivotal point. I had to stand my ground even if it meant that we took hit a financially. It was going to be a change that would affect our whole family, but my happiness was worth the price. I would sacrifice mocha coffees, eating out, and vacations. I wouldn't need any of those things if I was passionate about my career. Maybe it seemed selfish to Scott, but I was doing this for our family. I wanted to be an example to our children, showing them they had the power to create the life they wanted. Now, it was up to Scott to decide what he wanted. *Would he choose to support me and my happiness or decide to keep the house he had built?*

I collected myself and bravely walked back to the table. While I was gone, the food had arrived, but I couldn't eat. I asked the waitress to box up my whole meal. Scott was staring at me, waiting to hear what I had to say.

I calmly said, "You are either choosing me and my happiness or a house you built. If you are choosing the house, I think there is a bigger conversation we need to have."

He stared at me like he didn't know this side of me.

I continued, "And if you do this, I need you to be completely on board. You can't hold it against me if things don't work out well."

He paused for a few seconds and said, "OK." Scott is a man of few words, but I knew his simple "OK" meant I could count on him for support no matter the outcome. We were in this together.

He had a lot of questions, and I had very few answers. As we sat in the Olive Garden that rainy night, I told him that I would get a part-time job, maybe waitressing.

I said, "I don't know how this will work out. It just will." And I believed it would.

I don't think it matters if you are four years old or forty years old. You want your parents to be proud of you. My parents both worked in the school district I attended. For all four years of high school, my dad was my principal. In the hallways, he was the first one to hear about the student skip days and who was planning to throw parties on the weekend. A couple of times, I remember cringing, knowing I was in trouble when I heard my name and *"come to my office"* over the PA system.

Being in the same school wasn't all bad though. He did the scheduling for every student in the school and always gave me a sneak preview of my classes. When I was in 9th grade, he put me in a Speech class that was a requirement for all college-bound students. The first day of class, I realized I was the only freshman of juniors and seniors. I was terrified of public speaking, on top of being in front of upper classmen. I pleaded with my dad to change my schedule, and he agreed to take me out of the class but said I would have to take it my junior year. I was happy to delay it, but my experience turned out only slightly better my junior year. I developed hives every time I spoke and had to leave the room to catch my breath when I was done.

There were other benefits to being in the same school. I was grateful when I needed lunch money or I left a book at school and needed to get into my locker on the weekend. People always asked, "*How was it having your dad as your principal?*" I didn't think it was terrible or wish it to be different. It was all I knew.

My mom taught kindergarten. I had stopped in her room many times over the years and even spent a day shadowing her in high school. I witnessed the maternal bond she had with her students when she held their hands as they walked through the halls, wiped their noses, and genuinely smiled as they rushed in the room. I admired the kind of teacher she was. I just never felt the way she did.

Having spent almost their entire careers working for the same school district, it was going to be challenging for my parents to see my point of view.

"What was wrong with teaching?" they asked.

I wanted to explain to them that there was nothing wrong with any of the grade levels I taught, or my school district, or teaching in general, it just wasn't right for me. I just hadn't quite figured out how to put it into words—because I hadn't figured out yet what I wanted to do next.

I wanted them to say it was OK and give me their blessing to quit. Of course, I didn't need their permission, but I wanted their validation and encouragement. When I told them our plan, they were too worried to be supportive. My parents didn't want to see us struggle. They wanted the best for us.

"What are you going to do for income and insurance? Your family depends on you for support."

They were right. At the time, I was the breadwinner. I still didn't have a clear career path, but I knew I would do whatever I needed to make it work.

A few days later, my dad called me. He had been so concerned about me not having a new job that he had talked to some friends of his and learned of an opening in a corporate position. It involved planning large group functions, working in an office, and a lot of traveling. He estimated the pay would be about the same as teaching, but I would work the whole year. The position needed to be filled right away, so if I was hired, I would quit teaching immediately, before the school year ended.

Having a job with a similar salary would definitely ease Scott's financial concerns. We wouldn't have to sell our house or move the kids out of our neighborhood away from all their friends. Taking this job would also relieve my parents' worries too. I started to create an updated résumé and cover letter.

The possibility of leaving teaching was exciting, so I called Janie to tell her about it. As I started telling her about the position and how I had sent a résumé, I had the feeling I was trying to talk her and myself into the position.

Janie said just one word: "Nylons."

I had told her I didn't want to wear nylons and be stuck working in an office with an inflexible schedule. This was the first opportunity to transition to the career of my dreams, and I was seriously considering a position where I would need to dress professionally, work in an office, and have less time with my family. These were all things on my "Don't want" job list. I didn't really want this job; I was searching for an easy way out that would take away all this stress and anxiety about the future. I was so worried about making everyone else happy that I had been ready to sell myself short again. Janie was right. I needed to hold out for what was right for me. *Nylons* became the word we used to mean selling out or settling. I had come this far, and I deserved to have a career I was passionate about. I just needed to figure out my purpose.

---

### *What's important to you?*

*What are the top three things that are most important in your life?*

*1.*

*2.*

*3.*

- *Do you show these things are most important by giving them your time and energy?*
- *Allowing something to take up your space that really doesn't serve you means there is less time and space for things that bring you joy.*

---

# CHAPTER SIX

# *Evaluate Everything*

Analyze what's in your space.

Things don't stay because they have always been
there; they have to earn their place in your life.

After almost eighteen years, I was quitting the only
career I had ever known. It was exhilarating and
terrifying at the same time. For so many years, I had
wanted to quit. It was hard to believe it was finally
happening.

There were so many good memories at
school with Leslie and Amy. We taught together for
five years. For Halloween, we were The Three Little
Kittens Who Lost Their Mittens. On the one
hundredth day of school, we wore grey wigs and
polyester outfits we bought from Goodwill to dress
up like we were one hundred years old. Each year, in
November, we prepared an entire Thanksgiving
dinner with our students: turkey, stuffing, mashed
potatoes, and pumpkin pie. The three of us came in at
5:30 am to put the turkeys in roasters and went for

breakfast until school started. When I organized a district wide 5K, even though neither one of my friends were runners, they did the whole course with me—in the rain. I sat with them at every in-service meeting, laughing at our inside jokes and making the best of the long days. I certainly wouldn't miss the meetings, but I was going to miss my team.

Amy was the first to know about my plan to quit teaching. I told her at an in-service training a week before school started. She was interested to hear how I came to my decision. I excitedly told her about my brainstorming and list writing, making her promise not to tell anyone.

A few days later, while we were getting our rooms ready for the beginning of school, I walked across the hall into Leslie's classroom and closed the door. I didn't want anyone to overhear me telling her it would be my last year teaching.

With tears in her eyes, she hugged me and said, "I am going to miss you, but I know this is what you want."

Leslie was only a few years older than Amy and I, but she always mothered us. I was the youngest, Leslie nicknamed me "Baby."

Once she knew about my plan to quit teaching, she started covertly counting down the "last" of every school function I would ever do as a teacher. As the year progressed, she pretended to capture each moment with an invisible camera. At the school Christmas concert, she focused me in her fake camera, pretended to snap a picture, and then whispered, "Baby's last Christmas Concert" and smiled at me. There was "Baby's last Valentine party," and "Baby's last spring conferences." It was our little secret. It was heartwarming to have her support and see how genuinely happy she was for me.

All year long, without the staff knowing, I purged files and left unneeded supplies in the faculty room in preparation for my final days. In March, I submitted my required letter of intentions to my school district for the following year, making them aware for the first time of my plan to retire. The district compiled a list of potential openings and posted them in the main office for everyone to view. Teachers waited with anticipation to see which teachers were leaving and what grade levels would have vacancies. News always spread quickly through the building.

The day the list was posted, I was hiding in my room. Leslie, Amy, and I sat around my table, pulling out all the shamrocks and rabbits from the endless confetti bucket for our spring projects. I was staying away from the teacher's lounge and copy room to avoid running into other teachers. I wasn't ready to face all their questions. Teachers rarely resigned before retirement, and the few who did leave typically stayed home with their newborn or transferred with a spouse's job. No one just left. This list would thrust me and my decision to leave into the spotlight. I feared my resignation would immediately become the topic of conversation at school, and I was right. People were curious and wanted to know why I was leaving.

"Is she sick? Is everything OK at home?" they'd asked my team when I wasn't around.

Some asked me, "Why are you doing this *now*? Your children aren't even home anymore."

It was true. I had wanted to be home years ago before my children started school. *What if I had waited too long?*

Another coworker asked, "Where are you going to work? If you quit, you know you're never going to get another teaching job."

They brought up every fear I had about leaving, making me doubt if I should follow through with my plan to quit without having something else comparable lined up. In the beginning, I had been so sure that leaving was the right choice for me now, but the whole school year had been a roller coaster of emotions. It seemed like the odds were against me.

One morning when I walked into my classroom, I was overwhelmed by the pressure of all the unknowns I was facing. I ran across the hallway into Leslie's room. She was sitting at her desk, working on her laptop. I burst into tears as I rambled about the fears I had. I was so afraid of failing. People thought I was crazy for willingly giving up a desirable teaching position without having secured another job. Maybe they were right. Maybe I shouldn't do it.

Leslie cried as she hugged me and said, "It is not what everyone would or should choose, but it's what's right for you." She reminded me that this was my path and what I wanted. I wasn't trying to get everyone to quit. They didn't need to agree with my choice. Scott and I were the only people who needed to be OK with our decision.

I had turned forty just a year before. Maybe my increasing age was the reason I began scrutinizing my life. *Was I using my time wisely?*

It was my nature to be moving and busy. As I slowed down and spent more time thinking and journaling, I realized I actually raced through most of my days. Speeding through unloading the dishwasher and grocery shopping, I tried to cram one more chore or errand into each day, falling into bed exhausted each night. My thought was that if I finished all the chores that day, the next day I would relax. The only problem was that by the next day, I thought of ten more things that needed to be done and added them to my list. *Why was I always rushing? Why was I so busy?*

I didn't realize how hectic our lives had become. The family calendar was packed with so many sports and social functions that I had to write some of them outside the daily blocks, drawing arrows for all the events that didn't fit. It was so full one winter that I hoped for a blizzard. I wanted so much snow that the governor of Pennsylvania would issue a state of emergency where the roads were closed and only emergency personnel were allowed to drive. School, sports, and all activities would be postponed, and we would be forced to stay at home.

I craved time at home, but short of weather-imposed cancellations, I hadn't figured out how to make it a reality. Each time we received an invitation, I allowed the calendar to decide what we would do. If the calendar was open that day, we accepted even if it wasn't something we really wanted to attend. Sometimes, I even agreed to go to multiple parties or activities held on the same day, dragging the kids from one event to the next, none of us really enjoying any of them. I badly needed to take control of my schedule and cut out some of the clutter.

I saw that I took on more than I should because I didn't want to let people down. I thought I would look selfish if I didn't help out.

When I was asked to coach, I rationalized that since I had played basketball, I was obligated to accept the position. With weekly practices, games, and emails with parents, coaching is a huge time commitment. I spent a great deal of time and energy on it, and I didn't enjoy it. I led the team out of a sense of duty, but there is so much more to coaching than having the skills needed and the time available.

I decided an essential requirement for me to accept any volunteer position in the future was I had to *want* to do it.

I also reflected on my friendships. We spent a lot of time with families in our neighborhood. It was easy to get together because our children were friends, and we lived a few houses away. I wondered if we were just friends because of convenience. *If I moved further away, would our kids still be friends? Would we still get invited to parties?* Our move would be a test of many of my friendships.

I needed supportive friends who would be there for me as I grew. I had no idea what our future would hold with all the changes. It was always painful when a friendship ended. Looking back at past friendships, some didn't continue because they weren't that strong. If I held on tight to friendships that didn't work anymore, I couldn't be open for new friends to enter my life.

I continued evaluating different career options, and professional organizing kept showing up as a theme in my life. Throughout my years teaching, I changed grade levels and buildings and often ended up in a classroom of a recently retired teacher. The rooms were abandoned while cupboards and drawers remained packed full. I spent days clearing out their supplies so I could move in my own. I loved the "treasure hunt" of discovering what lay hidden in each cabinet. I uncovered quantities of construction paper, hole reinforcers, and jugs of paint that were more than I could use in a decade. I had fun redistributing the extra supplies to other teachers who needed them. In one classroom, I found twenty-five hole punches and staplers. I happily carried them to the office and asked if I could exchange them for a bottle of Wite-Out and a box of glue sticks.

I used any free time I had to organize my room. Rarely, on an in-service day, we would be permitted time to work in our rooms. Other teachers knew my love of organizing and asked if I would help reorganize their cabinets. I started saying I was creating a "healthier space," and other teachers wanted that too. Organizing the room gave me a calm, focused feeling, but it wasn't just organizing my room that made me feel calm and focused—I thought back to when I organized my basement.

We lived next door to one of Scott's model homes that he used as an office. To help people better visualize the house, we staged it with kitchen and dining room tables, lamps, and plants. In the past, customers had liked walking through our staged homes so much that they decided to buy it instead of building a new one.

We had an unfinished basement in our home where we stored some of the furniture from our previous basement. When a model home sold, we kept all the furniture to stage the next home. Instead of renting a storage unit, we walked all the furniture across the yard and down into our basement, adding to the couches, bar stools, and TVs that were already there. We had more than eighteen wooden chairs, four tables, two desks, and filing cabinets. All of it stacked on top of each other, turning our basement into a furniture graveyard.

One weekend, I had a brainstorm to reorganize the basement to be functional instead of just storage. I started by laying all the extra throw rugs and carpets on the concrete floor. I imagined different zones for various activities. I pushed a couch, end tables, and TV to one side and created a hangout area for the kids. I used the desks and filing cabinets to make an office/study area. In the last area, I used the various tables and chairs to transform the space into a large bar area with darts and a slot machine. I worked by myself for hours, inspired and driven to transform our storage into usable space.

Over the years, I talked about my organizing projects like the basement with my friends and family. They commented on how much I enjoyed it and wondered if I would help them. I usually didn't take any money. It was just fun.

One summer, my friend Kris, from book club, called to tell me she was ready to move into the new house she and her husband had built. She wanted to unpack everything and offered to pay me to help organize her kitchen, some closets, and utilize her space efficiently.

We started the next week on a hot, August day, and Scott took the kids to the pool. Usually, I hated to miss out on doing anything with my family, but this was different. After all, there would be other days to go to the pool. It wasn't every day I had the chance to organize.

The first day, I spent six hours unpacking and arranging dishes and kitchen items in the cabinets or back into boxes to be donated. Kristine commented that I didn't stop to eat or go to the bathroom for hours. I was so engaged in what we were doing that the hours flew by. I had been doing a lot of physical work on a hot day, but as I left her house, I was energized. Excitedly, I went home and told Scott all about what we did. It didn't feel like work at all.

The following week, I attended a school in-service day. By contract, there were two required meeting days in the summer, and a third day was optional for pay. These days were typically used to learn about new or updated curriculum that would be implemented the next year.

It was a rainy summer morning when I arrived at the elementary school. The day started with the usual coffee and pastries and catching up with teachers I hadn't seen since summer started. Then at 8:30 am, we sat down at cafeteria tables for training. I looked at the clock repeatedly; time moved so slowly. I counted the hours left and hoped the instructor would let us out early.

Before 9:00 am, I started to plan where my colleagues and I might go for lunch, which was the highlight of my day. The worst part of the day was knowing that I typically rated in-service days as more enjoyable than school days spent in the classroom, and those days would be starting soon. When the training ended, I gathered up my things and hurried to my car, happy to be leaving.

I drove to pick up Natalie, who had spent the day at a friend's house.

"How was your day?" she asked.

"Long and tiring." I wondered how I could be exhausted from sitting all day.

"It's too bad you don't get paid for your in-service today," she said.

"I actually do get paid," I said.

"Oh, really. How much?"

I was stunned to realize I earned the same amount of money doing the in-service training as I did when I organized for Kristine. I had always thought of organizing as a hobby, something fun, not really a career.

Reflecting back to that time nearly a year before, I remembered how inspired and full of energy I was after my six hours of organizing. It was so drastically different from how I felt at the end of every school day. *Could organizing be my passion?*

I needed to learn more about how to start and run a business. I googled information about organizers and their average fees. I bought a book about launching, managing, and growing an organizing business. Being an organizer sounded like a good fit for my personality, but I couldn't tell if I really wanted to become an organizer or if it would just be an escape from teaching.

I related it to being in a bad relationship: I've seen friends in relationships where they weren't happy, but they didn't do anything about it until a new person came along. Often, the new person wasn't better; they were just different. They offered an option to flee the bad relationship, but in the end, the new person wasn't right either. Was I just latching onto another career to save me from this one? Would I be happy with professional organizing in a few years, or would I be eager to get out?

---

### *Busy, Busy, Busy*

*Clutter is anything that weighs you down. We mostly talk about the physical things that occupy our space, but too much of anything can be overwhelming. Being overscheduled is a way we clutter our time.*

- *What are you busy doing?*
- *Does it bring you joy?*
- *What could you cut out so that you have more time for what you want to do?*

# CHAPTER SEVEN

# *Saying Goodbye*

Change is an inevitable part of life.

We pushed the red and white FOR SALE sign in the yard, making the public announcement that we were moving. It wouldn't be long before our neighbors started asking us where we were going. We didn't have an answer. We still hadn't found any houses that were cheap enough, but I was excited that spring had just started—the best time to sell a house.

I focused my energy on something I could control: getting our house ready for potential buyers. I thoroughly cleaned, knowing people would be opening drawers and closets and critiquing every inch.

Since Scott had built the house and I had always enjoyed showing our homes, I held an open house most Sunday afternoons. I bought tulips for the kitchen and balloons to tie to the open house signs. I walked through the house turning on all the lights, hopeful that someone would love our house as much as we did. Week after week, I walked families through the rooms, wondering which one might buy our home.

The kids protested against us moving anywhere outside of our neighborhood. Even though we looked at houses in different towns, Scott and I decided we didn't want to put them through the added stress of changing schools, so we decided to limit our search to homes in our town.

A Victorian-style house with painted exterior woodwork came up in our search. When we went to look at it, we were drawn to high ceilings, a beautiful staircase, and the tall wavy glass windows. I looked at a bedroom with a chandelier hanging from the ceiling and imagined it becoming Natalie's new room. I knew we would have to downsize, but I wasn't sure how we would fit our family's stuff into the small Victorian closets. The few closets that did exist were so shallow that a hanger had to be angled sideways for the door to close. It was so different from the new homes we had always lived in. It certainly would be a challenge, almost like living in a "tiny house."

Scott kept looking on real estate sites, and he spotted a new listing. It was an older house and priced really low. There were only pictures of the outside, which is a telltale sign that a house is in bad shape and needs a lot of work.

We went to meet Danielle, the realtor, at a house on Spruce Street the next day. We got there early and sat in the car, taking in the 1920's craftsman style red brick home with a large front porch. The shrubbery was overgrown, and the roof sagged.

After a few minutes in the car, we got out and walk around to see the side of the house. The small yard was taken up by an oversized wishing well. There was no water, but the inside revealed several large cracks and broken tiles. The yard reminded me of the disrepair that had fallen on Miss Havisham's home in Dicken's *Great Expectations*.

As we walked up to meet Danielle at the front door, I had to step carefully to avoid tripping on the broken concrete walkway that surrounded the house.

Danielle typed in the code on the lockbox and asked, "Are you ready?"

"Yea, we can't wait to see inside." We smiled in anticipation, but as the door opened, our smiles quickly faded. We were hit with a strong, foul odor.

"Oh, it doesn't smell as bad as it did the last time I was here," Danielle said.

The house had a thick smell like the windows had been closed for years. Animal fur, mouse droppings, and rotten food were immediately visible. No one lived in the house, but the sink and countertops were full of dirty dishes and food that had been left out. Cabinet doors hung crooked off their hinges, and countertops were covered in something that looked like wallpaper.

As we walked through the house, we saw newspapers, mail, and trash in several areas of the house, and some piles were waist deep. A radiator had exploded, causing water damage in one area, and the ceiling was hanging in another room due to a roof leak. We walked around overwhelmed, imagining all the work it would take to turn this mess into a home.

The house had only been on the market for a few days, but Danielle told us that another buyer was writing up an offer that night. Unless we were ready to put in a bid, we would lose out. We were in shock of the magnitude of disrepair in the house. Buying it would mean a total renovation, which was not something we had ever done before. We weren't ready to take it on, and the price was high for all the work that needed done. We would have to pass on the Spruce Street house. We weren't too disappointed. We had just started looking anyway.

We continued to look for houses that spring. Scott now had his teaching degree and was substituting and waiting for a position to open. I watched as he longed for a classroom of his own. I wished we could swap places. I knew I didn't want to spend another year teaching. My life's purpose was on my mind all the time.

When Leslie, Amy, and I sat and talked at lunchtime, the latest Oprah's *SuperSoul Sunday* was often the topic of conversation. I loved sharing what Oprah Winfrey and her guests said about finding your passion and purpose. Oprah feels it is your job in life to figure out your passion and purpose. I remember hearing her say, "*Do what you love, and the money will follow.*" I repeated this sentence in my head like a mantra, hoping it would guide me to my purpose. As long as we could afford to pay our bills, I was not concerned about money.

I cried when one guest, Bishop T. D. Jakes said, "*Let your passion lead you to your purpose, and when you find your purpose, the dam of your life floods over.*" I wanted to feel that kind of passion about my career, to have an undeniable feeling of purpose. To be able to lose myself in my work, not watching the clock or counting the days until retirement.

But I was so fearful of jumping into the wrong career. I needed more time to figure out my passion. I decided I should get a temporary job.

I had started waitressing when I was fifteen. My mom drove me to my first job at Dempsy's, a diner style restaurant. I was trained to take orders, prepare side dishes, and deliver everything to the customers. I hadn't waitressed in a restaurant for over ten years, but as a mom, I had years of experience serving hot plates of food to picky eaters. It wouldn't take me long to get back into the swing of waitressing.

I talked with a coworker at school who was a part-time banquet waitress at a local high-end hotel.

"You should apply. It's good money," she said.

I was relieved when I was hired. Now I would have a way to earn money when my teaching salary stopped. The first step was to attend a training session where I learned about the high standards and morals expected from the company.

In the last weeks of my final school year, Leslie was chirping "Baby's last field day," "Baby's last full week," and "Baby's last Monday." She didn't have to whisper it anymore.

On the last day of school, I watched the other retiring teachers say goodbye to their students with tears in their eyes. I heard them tell colleagues, "I don't know what I'm going to do, I'm going to miss teaching."

When I dismissed the class for the last time, I walked into my empty room and surveyed it one final time. I didn't feel sad at all; I felt relieved. I was finally done, and there were so many new adventures waiting for me. I could skip out of the building and never look back, but every year, there was a final staff luncheon where retiring teachers were honored, sometimes with a touching video montage or speeches from colleagues. I knew my friends wanted to wish me well, but I didn't like that kind of attention. I hated opening gifts in front of everyone at my baby shower and stopped attending a birthday club right before I would be the guest of honor.

Leslie found a unique way to give everyone the chance to say goodbye and help me along my journey. She asked staff members to write an inspirational quote or message on poster board, and she took a picture of them holding it. She scrapbooked the pictures and presented the book to me with just a few words at the luncheon. Leslie's thoughtfulness and support brought tears to my eyes. I was going to miss her. She had succeeded in creating the perfect, peaceful ending to my teaching career.

## *How to Make Your Own Quote Book*

- *Search Pinterest or magazines to find quotes that motivate you, empower you, or bring you joy.*

- *"Pin" the quotes on a virtual board or print and cut them out to display.*

- *Quotes can be arranged on thick paper to display, in an album, or put on a bulletin board.*

- *Use the quotes to inspire you or help you get through tough times.*

CHAPTER EIGHT

# *A New Path*

Try to remain positive when making changes in your life.

It really didn't hit me the first few weeks of summer that I didn't have to go back to school—it was over. Early in June, our family usually went to the beach. We had been making the yearly trip to the Outer Banks or Virginia Beach with my parents and my sister's family for over a decade. The rates were always cheaper the beginning of summer, so we could afford to rent a huge house where everyone could stay together.

This year, Scott and I were trying to save money and decided it would be better if we didn't go. I was disappointed, but this was one of the sacrifices I was going to have to make. I was scheduled to get trained that week so that I could start waitressing right away. I needed to work as much as I could this summer to make up for the teaching paycheck I wouldn't be getting in the fall.

My first day of training, I dressed in my stiff white dress shirt, black blazer, and pants. The uniform included a necktie, which Scott tied for me. With my hair pulled back, I set out, eager to learn the ropes at my new job. I was excited to start something completely different, and I looked forward to the physical work.

When I arrived, I smiled and said, "Hi," to everyone. There were few smiles in return and barely any eye contact. The only looks I got in return were ones of skepticism, and then I heard the whispers.

"Who is that?"

"Why did they hire someone?"

"Who has to train her?"

I stood by myself, trying not to feel self-conscious as no one talked *to* me. I only knew the one coworker from my school, and she wasn't on that morning.

An older woman was assigned to train me. There was no small talk or getting to know each other as she quickly walked around gathering things and seemed annoyed to have me trailing behind her. I was happy when the shift ended and figured it was just awkward because it was new. *The first day is always hard, tomorrow would be better.*

When I arrived for the second day of training, I was optimistic. *I can do this.* I walked in and looked for the woman who trained me the day before, but I didn't see her.

One of the waitresses turned to me and said, "Who's training you today?"

"I'm not sure. I thought I'd have the same trainer as yesterday."

"She's not scheduled today."

The staff started talking to each other, and it was obvious no one wanted to train me.

I stepped to the side when another veteran server, who looked to be about my age, stomped in a few minutes later. She slammed her keys and ID badge down on the counter. Everyone stared at her.

"I just got back from vacation. Why do I have to train her?" she complained to the room.

I felt so uncomfortable, and I fought back tears. It was only the beginning of my second day, and it was off to a terrible start. Being new, I was still learning and needed help. I felt so vulnerable. There was always someone watching me and commenting on any mistake I made. I wanted to do well, but when I asked my trainer a question, she replied in a short, condescending tone, implying I should already know the answer. I worried about doing anything wrong, and my stomach was in knots from the moment I arrived. *How am I going to work here?*

Suddenly, it made sense why there were openings for this job: it was a tough work environment. *I left a comfortable teaching position where I had friends, made a good salary, and was treated with respect. What if I can't make enough money at another job, and I have to work here?* I thought about when there had been substitute teachers in my building. I knew I hadn't been cruel or talked about them but hoped I had been helpful and made them feel welcome.

The training shifts were hard. The hours were long, the staff was unfriendly, and the whole time I was thinking about how I missed out on our family beach vacation. After a week, I finished the training, and I could finally start making tips. As awful as the job was, I needed it. I had to suck it up. *You need to be positive and find something to be grateful for each shift.*

I arrived really early for my first real shift with tips. I was so worried about being late. I wandered around and peeked into the ballroom. I stood watching the florists who were busy placing beautiful arrangements full of perfect pale roses around the room. It looked like they were preparing for a fairy tale wedding. I inhaled the scent of the flowers filling the room and hoped I would be working this event. I would love to see the cake and watch the couple's first dance together. I had tears in my eyes just thinking about it.

Two servers walked in the room talking to each other. One said, "I just saw the bride and groom taking pictures out on the lawn. I bet they'll be divorced in a year."

I shuddered at her cynicism.

"We better go to the pantry for the pre-shift meeting," the other one said.

I followed them into the narrow area and stood off to the side, trying not to be seen.

The captain made up a floor plan for each event and announced the waitressing pairs. As she started to read off the names, I looked around the room and could tell by the looks the servers were giving each other that a few were hoping not to have me as a partner. I knew I wasn't as quick as the other servers yet, but I would work twice as hard.

I saw a waitress rush in. She had short blonde hair and blue eyes. I hadn't met her yet, but she turned my direction, mouthed "Hi," and smiled. I was stunned. It was the only genuine smile I had received since I started working there.

"Laura and Rhonda, you are working the event outside."

I felt relieved when I found out the new girl was my partner, and we would get to escape the criticizing eyes of the full-time staff for the day.

As we set up our equipment, Rhonda and I talked. She had not worked there long but had similar negative experiences. She explained that since we worked banquets, the gratuity was pooled together and split among the servers. The full-time staff were opposed to new hires because it impacted their wages.

While we served sandwiches for the afternoon, I learned that Rhonda had been in a professional career. She explained that she only planned to waitress temporarily, while she shifted careers. We had so much in common. I decided to tell Rhonda I was starting my own business and the name of it, Healthier Spaces Organizing. I was grateful to have made an ally at work.

As the summer continued, I was only scheduled for a handful of waitressing functions. Since the kids were home for the summer, I didn't mind. I knew I could wait a few more weeks, but if work didn't pick up in the fall, I would have to find a new job.

In the meantime, Scott and I kept searching for houses. Every house on the market cost too much, and we needed something inexpensive, a fixer upper. We started to regret not making an offer on the craftsman style house on Spruce Street. It had been much less than all the other houses we saw, and buying it would have allowed us to cut our expenses.

The Victorian house seemed like the second best option. We went back to visit it two more times, taking the kids with us and really trying to imagine our lives there. Storage was a big concern. Our oversized couches and chairs weren't going to fit in the small Victorian rooms, so we would probably have to buy new furniture. Scott had plans drawn for new kitchen cabinets and started adding up the costs of repairs we would have to make to the house. It looked like we might not end up saving anything if we moved here. We started to worry. We had to downsize our expenses, or we were going to end up in financial trouble.

It was July when the realtor with the Spruce Street house called. "Sorry I couldn't call you earlier, but the house was under negotiations. I can talk to you now because the buyers backed out."

We hadn't talked to Danielle in four months.

"So, the house is back on the market?" I asked, hopefully.

"Well, there is an agreement with the bank to get it at a reduced rate, but you have to settle by the end of this week. I wanted to let you guys know first. If you're interested, I won't show it to anyone else."

We were so surprised and hopeful. Since we had passed on the Spruce Street house, we had been comparing it to each house we saw and were certain that we had lost out on a good chance. Although the house needed a lot of work, the price was right. We went to see it right away. We only had a few days to make our decision.

The house hadn't changed at all since we had seen it a few months before. The piles of trash were still there, the ceilings hung low, and huge renovations were needed everywhere. But for the first time, we could see it had good bones. Months before, we had been so overwhelmed by the smell and number of repairs needed that we hadn't fully appreciated the character of the house. Scott noticed the tall original wood baseboards throughout the house, and I loved the glass door knobs and curved archway.

The former owners were deceased, so the house was vacant which allowed us access to use the lockbox and walk through it every day over the next week. While Scott added up the repairs we would need to do, I restrained from straightening up. The Spruce Street house fit our budget and we could use lots of "sweat equity" for the remodeling to make it our home.

We told Danielle we wanted to buy the house. She explained the executor would be getting a dumpster to clear out everything because for a house to be sold in Pennsylvania, it needed to be able to be "broom swept." There were spaces in the house where we couldn't even see the floor. I remembered walking through seeing clothes still in their dry-cleaning bags and dozens of paperback books on the floors. There were so many things that someone else could use in the kitchen alone: glasses, a blender, and dishes.

My need to recycle and redistribute resources was strong. Against the advice of Scott and the realtor, I wanted to purchase the house "contents and all as is." That was the only way I could make sure everything didn't end up in a dumpster. Scott was reluctant to accept the house that way but agreed to let me clear it out as long as I didn't slow down all the remodeling he would be doing. We made a deal: I had to stay one room ahead of him. My mind was racing, thrilled by the challenge.

Danielle was happy that we were going to buy the house, but she had a strange request. The previous owner had been her sister-in-law's wedding photographer and had not given her family pictures they had paid for. She wanted to know if we could give them any pictures we found of their wedding. Looking around the house, I knew it would be like finding a needle in a haystack, but I told her I would keep my eye out for them.

The final walk-through was scheduled for the next day and we would sign the paperwork to make the house ours. I was so excited I hardly slept the whole night. For so many months, this huge life change had only been in my mind, a vision. Once we bought the house, there would be a tangible sign that our lives were changing. Buying the house was a key step in our plan to downsize. I felt alive! As soon as Scott's eyes opened in the morning, I immediately started talking about the plans I had devised for cleaning out the house. I had not felt this moved by a project in a long time.

Since the house was bank owned, we had an agreement, and we felt no last-minute jitters about someone backing out. We had seen the house in complete disrepair, and we were taking it "as is."

We met Danielle for the routine walk through before settlement, and we invited Brian along, the realtor who sold our home, thinking he would appreciate seeing the construction of the house and the potential it held. Before walking in, we forewarned him about the condition of the house, the smell, and the trash covering the floor and areas where it was impassable.

Immediately as we walked around, we noticed things were different. The stove was missing. There was a vacant spot where it had been each time we had walked through the house. Wires were hanging out of the walls in the living room, a telltale sign that sconces were ripped from where they hung. A huge wooden desk looked like it had been smashed with a sledgehammer, and new trash bags sat blocking the side entrance. Our hearts sank as we walked through the house and saw that it had been ransacked. The one-hundred-year-old American Chestnut doors and trim were gouged and many of the antique glass doorknobs lay broken on the floor.

We had allowed the executor to take family keepsakes and pictures, but we learned he had given the lockbox code to his relatives. The night before our walk through, these people weren't just taking mementoes; they were caught by the police stealing radiator covers, filing cabinets, and other metal. They had to return the few items they had in their truck at that time, but since we hadn't inventoried of the contents when we walked through, we had no idea what things they had taken before they were caught. We couldn't press charges against them either because we didn't own the house yet.

Scott was so angry. It wasn't about the mess they made, the smashed furniture, the bags of trash brought in, or even whatever items were stolen. In order to completely remodel the house, we needed to clear everything out anyway. We didn't know what they stole, except an old stove that we would have gotten rid of, so it wasn't much of a loss. What upset

Scott was the irreparable damage to the wood that upset him. Our hearts were heavy. It was the woodwork that gave the house its character, one of the few parts of the house we wanted to preserve. In the 1950s, the American Chestnut tree went extinct, so replacing these original wood features of the house would be unlikely or extremely expensive.

Now we had a decision to make: the offer from the bank would run out in a few hours. Our options were to continue with the sale with a little money off or walk away. We knew the houses that were on the market, and we liked this one and couldn't let it slip through our fingers. On that hot July afternoon, we bought the house.

Scott and I were exhausted from the complications with the settlement. We had planned to start working on the house early the day after we signed the papers when it was cooler and there was more daylight. With the recent problems with the extended family having access to the house, it was crucial to replace the locks immediately.

We walked into our new house, and the heat of the late afternoon made the pungent smell of rotting food, mouse poop, dog urine, and spilled wine more intense.

In the living room, Scott walked over to a stack of newspapers that had been stuffed under a baseboard heater. Neither of us had seen that on all our walk-throughs. As he bent down to remove the papers, he realized the heater was turned on, extremely odd for late July. Maybe we were just being paranoid. To ease our fears, we looked in each room, trying to spot anything that looked unusual. It was difficult to notice if something was out of place since the whole house was trashed. In the back corner of the spare bedroom, we found an iron on the ironing board plugged in and turned on. It was strange neither of us had noticed that all the times we had been in the house. Most of the lightbulbs were burned out or the switches didn't work.

By this time, the sun was setting, and the house was getting dark. Scott walked over to a pile of newspapers that lay where the stove had been. He lifted up the stack and discovered a mousetrap. It was loaded and matches were placed in the spot where the trap would come down. Now we were starting to panic. Someone wanted to burn the house down. We found three fire hazards in a half hour. What if there were more we didn't find? We had owned our house for less than a day, and it could go up in flames. We had to call the police.

Scott started changing the lock on the front door while we waited for an officer to arrive and make a report.

I went to the kitchen and looked at the crooked cabinet doors that wouldn't stay closed and the countertop full of rotten food. That was where I wanted to start. One of my first big projects as a professional organizer was organizing our new house. I would get first-hand experience figuring out what to do with someone else's stuff. I filled trash bags with expired cans of tuna and spices. Some of the labels looked decades old. I opened the drawers and wiped out mouse droppings. As the kitchen began to look a little better, I realized I had forgotten to take pictures before I started. I had been so excited to start, I left my camera in the car.

When the policeman arrived, he knew about the situation that had occurred at our address the night before. He took our statement and said that because of the suspicious activity while he was on patrol, he would keep a close eye out for anything that didn't seem right. We felt slightly relieved.

Scott had installed the new lock in the front door and moved to the side entryway to replace that one. It had been a long, hot, emotional day, and as soon as Scott finished the lock, we would leave.

The dimly lit room had previously been used as an office, but now it looked unrecognizable. The large wooden desk I had planned to donate to charity sat smashed in the middle of the room. Drawers were all pulled out and strewn around, and large black contractor bags lay on top. Every inch of floor space was covered with small pieces that looked like they were dumped from a dozen junk drawers. Scott set to work in that room as I continued in the kitchen, regretting not bringing gloves to clean.

It was 10:00 pm when Scott called for help.

"I dropped a screw I need to finish installing the deadbolt, and I can't find it anywhere."

"Where do you think it fell?" I asked.

"I have no idea. I didn't hear it hit anything," he said.

I squatted down and started searching the floor. I sorted through thumbtacks, nails, and other small hardware to find screws. I held up each one to show Scott, hoping I had found the right one to fit the lock. Nothing had gone right the whole day, and now this? I unsuccessfully scrounged the floor for about fifteen minutes.

"Can you just go get one at home or go to Walmart and buy a new deadbolt system?" I begged.

The possibility that we could find that small screw with very little light in all that mess was very unlikely.

Scott was getting frustrated. He hadn't heard where the screw dropped, which made it even more difficult to know where to search. It could have hit any of the six contractor bags and bounced off, or it could have fallen inside. I was going to have to dig through these trash bags.

I opened the first bag and was surprised to see it contained hanging file folders, not trash like I expected. Suddenly, as I sat on the floor, a sense of calmness washed over me. I had the feeling that everything would turn out all right. A reassuring voice in my head said, "Buying this house was not a mistake, everything will work out"

I gently shook the folder, hoping the missing screw would fall out. When nothing came out, I started leafing through. I couldn't believe what I had found.

"This bag is full of wedding pictures." I said excitedly.

"We need to find that screw, we don't have time to look at pictures." Scott said.

Still searching for the screw, I looked at a handful of other files before I opened a file and saw the faces of my realtor's sister-in-law and her father.

"Oh my gosh, here is Danielle's sister-in-law."

It was a picture of her father escorting her down the aisle. He had recently passed away and I knew what those pictures would mean to her family. How amazing it was to uncover them on the first night, when we weren't even looking for photos. I felt like her father was giving us a nudge from heaven to find them. With all the trouble we had with the house being looted, trashed, and the arson attempts, finding those pictures felt like a good sign to me.

Scott was getting more annoyed by the minute. I asked him to think again about where he thought it might have fallen. He looked down for the first time and found the screw. It had fallen into his tool belt. He finished installing the new lock, and we locked up and went home hoping our house would still be there when we came back the next day.

The next morning, Scott and I were happy to find our house still standing when we arrived. I was driven by all the work that needed done and started going every day that I wasn't scheduled to waitress.

The kids were not happy about our plan to fix up the house and move in town. When Natalie saw the house for the first time, she ran out crying and screaming, "I am not living there." Ryan was used to having lots of friends on our block that he played with at the playset in our big yard and the basketball hoop in our driveway. Our new house didn't have a playset or basketball hoop and the yard was very small. He didn't want to move out of our home either. Although Zach didn't want to leave his friends, he had the best outlook.

He said, "It might be kind of interesting to be the new kid in the neighborhood. It will give me something to write about for an essay."

They complained about the smell, and all three of them started referring to the new house as "The Dump." I couldn't blame them.

## *Steps to Clean Out Your Cabinets*

- *Start by looking at dates and getting rid of expired spices and foods.*

- *If you have nonperishable food that is within the date, consider donating it to a food bank or shelter. Many places will also take fresh produce, which is helpful if your garden has an abundant crop or you have excess with a crop share program.*

- *Extra pet food can be taken to animal rescues.*

- *Give utensils you haven't found usable to charities.*

# CHAPTER NINE

# *Karmic Cash*

Letting go of things you don't need, brings the exact things you do need into your life.

News spread quickly through our small town about the purchase of our new house and its condition. Scott and I had lovingly nicknamed it "the hoarder house." People approached me in the grocery store and at picnics, fascinated with what they heard about the house. They offered to help us clean it out. After the initial interest of seeing the house wore off, I thought most people would have been overwhelmed by the smell and filth and ready to leave. There was a lot to do, and I couldn't waste time letting our house turn into a freak show. I was very selective with my volunteers; they had to be able to hang in for the long haul.

Scott began tearing down the walls and ceilings to reframe the house and update the electric and plumbing. He needed me to empty out each room—and quickly. Everywhere I turned there was an explosion of random items, nothing went together.

I had a lot of sorting to do. Without digging into the piles, I could see old newspapers, junk mail, and paper bags from fast-food restaurants. I moved closer to a mound and pushed it with my foot, exposing random clothing and paperback novels. There was no telling what I might find, like when I moved into the room of a retired teacher.

My mom volunteered to help me with anything I needed. We decided to clear out the master bedroom first. It was on the second floor, so we started early in the morning to get a jump on the humid, summer heat. We stood at the entrance of the small room, deciding where to start, the stench already overpowering the closed space. There were two small windows, but waist high piles and a broken Lazy Boy recliner prevented us from getting safely across the room to open them.

We noticed several cream-colored plastic bags in the room that were identical. When I looked inside, there was an empty box of Franzia white wine and a store receipt inside. I peered into bag after bag and saw each one contained the same thing.

My mom and I carried armloads of bags and boxes to the front porch where we had fresh air and room to work. We used utility knives to cut apart the cardboard wine boxes and cut out the spouts. Inside each box was a plastic bladder containing a small amount of wine. As we slashed the bags, the rancid, sticky liquid leaked out onto our legs and arms. The spouts and bladders went into the trash, and we piled the cardboard up to recycle.

In a few hours, with stacks of flattened cardboard covering the porch, we needed more space. Out of curiosity, I wondered how many boxes were coming out of our bedroom. We counted the stacks, loaded them into the minivan, and took them to the recycling center. My mom and I stood side by side slashing boxes apart and made two more trips to empty the cardboard. After a few days, I had lost count of the wine boxes around three hundred.

For the first time in eighteen years, as the calendar turned to August, I didn't feel a sense of dread. I was relieved knowing I wouldn't be headed back to the classroom. I was excited for the fall and hoped that with my family all at school, I would be more available to work with organizing clients. I had a handful of sessions each month but not enough.

I also wasn't getting many waitressing shifts, and I started to worry about our finances. In fact, I hadn't worked at all in five weeks. Coworkers said it was unusually slow and assured me the shifts would pick up in the fall.

Scott had interviewed a few times but didn't get hired for a teaching position. He would have to substitute when school started or try to get his aid job again.

It was disappointing that our house hadn't sold, despite having open houses almost every Sunday for more than four months. Now, we had two houses, and no bread winning job between the two of us. The only thing we could do was hope for the best and keep ourselves busy.

We had more than enough work to do at the new house. Scott asked his dad and two good friends to be a part of a regular building crew. The four of them went to the house each morning if they didn't have another commitment. Each one was skilled in construction. Almost every day, I brought or made lunch for everyone working on our house, but I had a variety of different jobs.

Often, I was the runner, loading up the Prius or minivan with building supplies from Home Depot. Other days, I was the cleanup crew, sweeping up saw dust, picking up scraps of wood, or rinsing out buckets of joint compound. My least favorite job was

125

"helper." It usually required me to stand in one spot and hand necessary supplies up to someone on a ladder. I found it difficult to just stand there. I wanted to wander off and *do* something, anything.

There were a lot of tedious jobs in the house, like pulling out all the nails and staples from the floor along the perimeter of each room. For several weeks, I sat on my knees in the kitchen with a heat gun. I warmed up small sections of a black tar-like substance on the floor and scraped it up with a putty knife. With these projects, I found these jobs almost meditative. I was in my own little world, humming to myself as I worked.

I regularly checked my cell phone for messages from potential organizing clients. I was mostly organizing for family, friends, and people I knew. I looked forward to organizing and was disappointed when people needed to cancel or reschedule.

My mother-in-law, Diane, came one day to help clean out the former office, the room where we had lost the screw. "What are you doing with these papers?" she asked.

"Putting all the junk mail and bills in this box to recycle." I explained.

There were so many stacks of paper on the floor that we sat sorting for hours until our bodies got stiff.

"What should I do with checks?"

"I can't cash them, so checks just get recycled too." As I grabbed another pile of mail, I added, "It would be nice to find a personal card because there might be cash inside it."

The first few pieces on the pile were junk mail that I threw into the recycle box. Then I spotted a lavender colored envelope, definitely not a bill. It was still sealed. I turned it over and saw the first name of the previous owner handwritten.

"This could be a personal card," I said as I tore it open. I read the front of the card aloud, "To my daughter on her birthday." Hopeful, I continued, "A mother could give her daughter cash..." I opened the card and inside was $25. Although it wasn't a lot of money, it felt like someone was listening to me and granting my wishes.

As I cleared out the house, I realized how many wedding photographs there were and how unlikely it had been that we managed to find our realtor's sister-in-law's pictures that first night. There were hundreds of files full of pictures in several rooms throughout the house, and I made sure to look at each one.

In each folder, I searched for pictures of the bride, groom, and wedding party to see if I recognized anyone. There were many pictures of families I knew and had grown up seeing in town. More than once, the pictures opened right to a photo of the father or mother of the bride or groom who I knew had recently passed. It was as if they were trying to send a message to their child. I decided to track down anyone I recognized in the pictures. It was extra work, but well worth the effort. They were so happy to get them back, and a few told me they had no other professional photographs from their special day.

I thought of myself as The Wedding Photo Fairy.

Each night before I left the house, I loaded up my vehicle with items that needed to leave: boxes full of paperback novels to deliver to our local library for their book sale, bags of clothing for the Salvation Army, unneeded building supplies to the Habitat for Humanity ReStore, and always a few files of wedding pictures. I loved planning out how to fit in all the deliveries with the other responsibilities on my list. While I drove around, I listened to the radio and belted out songs like "Happy" by Pharrell. With each load I gave away, I felt lighter.

Late afternoon, I drove back to our house to get Zach and Ryan for football. As they practiced with their team, I hurried back to the new house to organize for two hours before they needed to be picked up.

I moved items into my staging areas to be recycled, donated, sold, or saved. Any treasures I discovered, I moved to the fire place mantle to analyze later. The items I deemed "Mantle-worthy" ranged from coins and a wooden shoe form to family photographs and interesting shaped pieces of rusty metal. I was like an archaeologist, uncovering fragments of the lives that lived there before me.

I had a hard time tearing myself away from whatever I was working on at the house. I organized until the last possible minute and raced back, dirty and hot, to pick up the boys from practice. If Scott was able to pick up the boys, I kept working. Often, he would call me to tell me it was after 9:00 pm and I had lost track of time. I left exhausted each day but completely fulfilled. I had found my passion. I only wished I could have enough clients to be organizing full time.

During the last few weeks of the summer, we spent every minute at the house, trying to get as much work done as we could before school started.

Our friends and family stopped by to see us and check on the progress. Most were confused by the fact that we were selling our beautiful model home and choosing to move to a hoarded house. Although we had been working for weeks, the house was far from done.

As they pulled up to our new place, the first thing they saw was a toilet in the small front yard. The house was still full of stuff from the original owners, and with the construction, there was nowhere to put anything. We started to use the front porch as storage for extra doors, ladders, and building supplies that couldn't get wet. When we ran out of room on the porch, some things ended up in the yard around the house. One of the toilets needed to be moved to do some work, and the yard was the only place left to get it out of the way. After guests walked up the cracked sidewalk, they would see the green, threadbare indoor/outdoor carpeting on the porch floor and heaps of recovered trim leaning against the house. The screen door was broken, and on breezy days, it banged against the house.

Once inside the house, they were immediately hit by the stench, which sped up our tour. We walked up to see the bedrooms covered in trash, mouse droppings, and pet hair. As I showed our friends around our new house, I could see the disgust on their faces.

The main bathroom contained a toilet that looked like it had exploded. It was so repulsive that we covered the whole thing with an orange sheet that we found in the house. Next to the toilet was a knee high pile of foul-smelling rags and toilet paper with unknown stains that had been in the house when we bought it. For a while, no one had been brave enough to move it. I was quick to point out that we were fortunate to have another bathroom with a functioning toilet and explained our plans to transform the house. I was so excited about changing our lives, I didn't want them to feel sorry for us.

It was hard for most people to see our vision. Although my friends could tell I was happy, they found it difficult to relate to our situation. I could hear the concern in their voices when they asked us these questions:

"Did you sell your house?"

"So, you quit teaching. What are you going to do now?"

"Did Scott get a teaching job?"

When they learned we didn't sell our house, I was barely waitressing, and Scott didn't get a teaching job, they all had the same baffled look. "What are you guys going to do?"

"We are just throwing all the cards up in the air and seeing where they land," was my canned answer. There were so many unknowns with our plan, I had to stay positive. I couldn't find the words to tell them I was finally on the right path, exactly where I needed to be. Money was tight, but I was happy.

After all, it only took one person to buy our home and financially, things would be easier. Scott could still get a teaching position. There were always late resignations by teachers who wanted to extend their maternity leave or new classrooms created to accommodate increased summer enrollments. I prayed something would happen at the last minute for him and he would get a call. He deserved it. He was patient and wanted the best for the kids in our community.

I did everything I could to help out at Spruce Street except work on the roof. I was terrified of being up there and only assisted on the roof one time. After I got up, I was petrified to get down, paralyzed by the fear of slipping and falling off the roof. The week that Scott and his crew put on a new roof, I decided to work in the upstairs office so that I could be close if they needed anything.

There were shelves full of three-ring binders and more boxes of binders I had noticed in the attic. Each one was filled with plastic pockets. Most held either photo negatives or paper manuals. I threw away the negatives and recycled the paper but kept the binders. It was monotonous work, and because of the heat, everything was stuck to the plastic. The whole house was hot. We had a few fans, but I didn't like using them because they blew the papers around the room and made more of a mess.

I had refused to get a dumpster when we bought the house. I was determined to find homes for everything. Organizing guru Peter Walsh said: "*The good that you do with the stuff you don't need, I believe will come back in karmic ways.*" I love the term he uses for donating to others: Karmic Cash. I like connecting people with the resources they need. That was my plan for the binders. I posted them on a local Freecycle site, and a woman who was part of a homeschool consortium contacted me. I was still working to empty them, but she said she would take as many as we had. She planned to share them with thirty-two other families who would use them to organize their grade level curriculum. It felt good to stock up on Karmic Cash and keep things out of a landfill.

As Scott, his dad, and his friends bounced around on the roof, just hearing them above my head made me cringe. I continued to clear page after page in the binders. I had finished well over fifty with many still remaining when Scott's uncle poked his head in the office room. He was on his way up to check out the progress on the roof.

"What are you doing?" he asked as I sat on the floor surrounded by binders.

"I'm emptying these to give them to someone."

"Have you found any old baseball cards?" he asked, looking around the room.

"No, the previous owners didn't have kids."

He laughed and said, "You don't have to be a kid to collect baseball cards!"

Scott's uncle went out on the roof, and I went back to my job of emptying the binders.

I remembered going to flea markets with my family as a child. My parents would give my brothers, Chad and Brice, a few dollars to buy packs of baseball cards. Les and I weren't interested in the cards so they had to give us the hard, pink bubble gum sticks that came in each pack. I always felt like Les and I had the better end of the deal. Now, my brothers are grown men and I was pretty sure they still had their baseball card collections. Scott's uncle climbed out the second story window on to the roof and I went back to my job of emptying the binders.

About two hours later, I opened a red binder that from the outside didn't look any different from the dozens I cleaned out. But it was different, the clear pockets inside were full of old baseball cards. I didn't know much about them, but as I read the names, I was pretty sure that an early Jackie Robinson was a good find.

When Scott and the guys came off the roof, I couldn't wait to show them the collection. They told me we had a few valuable cards, including two Ted

Williams, rookie year. How amazing that I had gone through all those binders and found nothing exceptional, and then after Scott's uncle mentioned baseball cards, I uncovered some. Again, I felt an inner reassurance that we were being taken care of, and things would work out.

I had been happy the entire month of August, and the night before school started I felt light hearted. I never felt like that on a "school night." I had tried for so many years to change my path, and I worried that it was too good to be true. *Did I really do it?*

The next morning, I woke up early to take the traditional "First Day of School" pictures of Zach and Ryan on the front porch with their backpacks. Natalie wasn't in these pictures because she had won a scholarship to be an exchange student in France for the year. She wouldn't be going to our local high school, so instead of a picture with a bookbag, I took one of her pulling a suitcase. I could feel time slipping away with her. Not only was she leaving for France, but she was also growing up. I wanted to spend as much time with her as I could before she left.

The first morning of the school year, Natalie and I met Les at Starbucks. I felt like a kid playing hooky as the three of us drank mochas and ate salted caramel cake pops. This was what I had changed my career to do: spend quality time with my family.

Day after day, there was no word about any open teaching positions. Scott started substitute teaching, but he wasn't needed every day. I picked up a couple waitressing shifts a week, but it wasn't enough. I was excited each time clients called and booked a session, even if they were just friends and family so far. I looked forward to the days I could spend organizing and really wanted to grow my business.

Scott and I weren't making much money and had to pay bills for the house we were living in and expensive repairs for the new house. We tapped into our savings, and it was dwindling quickly. *How long could we afford to do this?* My decision to quit had put us in this situation. I hadn't been fired or lost my job; I made a choice to leave. What if it didn't turn out how I expected? *I can't go back to teaching.* I applied to pick up additional banquet waitressing shifts at a local conference center.

As the fall continued, our house had been on the market for seven months. We tried to spend as little money as we could on anything extra. A few weeks before my birthday, I told Scott that for my present, I wanted to have a yard sale with Les. It was so hard to spend time together. She worked full time and had three young kids, and I was working two jobs and trying to keep up with two houses. We sat talking and drinking hot chai lattes in camping chairs on the sidewalk while customers perused the tables full of stuff Scott had helped me carry out of the Spruce Street house. Les and I stayed there long after the last customer had left, laughing so hard I worried one of us might pee our pants. I made a little bit of money, cleared stuff from the new house, and had quality time with my sister. It was a perfect birthday gift.

By the time December arrived, I was really stressing about paying our bills. One night, I was tossing and turning in my bed and couldn't sleep. I quietly walked downstairs and pulled out a notebook. I wrote down all the bills that were due, like the new furnace for the Spruce Street house, the meager gifts we had purchased for Christmas, and our utilities. I saw in black and white that we were not going to have enough money in our account to pay for everything this month.

I panicked. We had always lived within our means and paid our bills on time, but now, our money was tied up in the houses. Worst of all, it didn't look like our situation would change any time soon. We were going into winter, a typically slow time for house sales, and most likely, Scott wouldn't get a teaching job until summer. I was overwhelmed thinking how long it would be until our finances could change and how little savings would be left. I had to come up with a way to make more money.

I started brainstorming ideas. The most obvious idea was to work more. I wanted to organize more, but I couldn't figure out how to get more clients. With banquet waitressing, even if I picked up every available shift, the gratuity lagged behind a few weeks, and I wouldn't get paid before the end of the month.

I made a list of furniture and trinkets from the new house I could sell on eBay or Craigslist. They would bring a little but still not enough. We found a lot of old pipes and metal around the house, so I would have to take them to the scrap yard to make some money. Luckily, I also still had the binder of baseball cards, and I could sell them. I also remembered someone I met that had "gold selling parties." I owned a few broken gold necklaces and gold earrings without a mate. It was not much, but it was worth a shot. I emailed her that night.

I googled "How to make money." Two of the options that came up were being an egg donor or a surrogate, but after a little research, I realized I was too old for both. Donating plasma was another item on the list. From a local website, I learned you could make $50 each time and up to $200 a month. I had been a blood donor since high school, so donating plasma seemed like a viable, but last option.

Although, I looked at the numbers and didn't think it was possible, I prayed that we would be able to pay our bills. I decided to host the gold party with my friends and family and was astonished when I made over a thousand dollars. Money started showing up in unexpected ways. We received a refund from our insurance company, and customers handed me personal tips when I was working banquets. When I was standing in the grocery store, trying to figure out how to stretch each dollar and make inexpensive meals, I would look down and notice a penny or dime on the floor. Finding coins didn't just happen once or twice, it seemed to happen almost every time I worried about money. Each coin I found felt like a personal message to me. *"Don't worry about the money; things will work out."* Someone was watching out for us. We were able to pay our bills that month.

# *Save, Sell, Donate, or Recycle?*

*Save: Is the item something you love or need? Don't ask yourself if you <u>could</u> use it; ask if you <u>will</u> use it. Listen to your gut. Learn to feel the difference between when you love something and when you are keeping it out of guilt. If it takes more than a few moments to decide, you probably don't really want or need it. If the item can be easily replaced, for under ten dollars, it's not something to worry about.*

*Sell: Is it worth the time and energy to sell? A few avenues to sell things are Craigslist, eBay, an auction house, or a consignment shop. Each one has its advantages and disadvantages.*

*Donate: If you don't choose to sell it, maybe it can be donated. Many organizations need our unwanted items. Some examples are Habitat for Humanity, Freecycle, Salvation Army, shelters, schools, religious organizations, food banks, libraries, and pet rescues.*

*Recycle: Most local communities offer recycling for glass, plastic, card board, and paper. Large appliance and office stores often have options for electronics. You can find a variety of mail-in programs across the country, by searching the web. Recycling scrap metal will even bring you a little extra cash.*

# CONSCIOUS PLACEMENT

It is important that things are not just shoved in a drawer. If you don't give careful consideration to where you place things, the space will not be functional and can quickly become cluttered.

Start by thinking about where and how often you use things. In the kitchen, pots and pans should occupy the cabinets closest to the stove where they are used. Items like holiday platters that are only brought out once a year can be stored farther away.

Think about the best location or "prime real estate" being the most convenient areas in each room. The kitchen has three locations with prime real estate: by the stove, by the sink, and by the refrigerator. In an office, prime real estate areas would be the desk top and the first few drawers. Make sure what occupies these spaces is essential for the work that is done there.

# CHAPTER TEN

# *Create the Space*

Consciously design the space to be functional for
your unique needs.

As winter started, we put all remodeling on hold at
Spruce Street. We couldn't afford both houses, and if
we couldn't sell our old house, we would have to put
the new house up for sale. Our family was in limbo,
wondering which house we would end up living in.
In early March, when our house had been on the
market for a full year, we finally received an offer. I
was relieved but held my breath that everything
would pass inspection and that the buyers wouldn't
back out.

If all went well, we would settle in two
months and move into town on Spruce Street.
Moving into town wasn't the path most people
chose. As their families grew and their careers
became more successful, they moved out of the town
and into neighborhoods like the one we were leaving.
Even people who lived in town were puzzled by our

decision and asked, "Why are you moving here?" It was hard to explain in one sentence.

What had started out as a change of careers had turned into much more. We weren't just downsizing our house—we were downsizing our whole lives. It was a lifestyle change, a conscious decision to cut down the amount of time we were spending in the car, driving the kids to practices, and running errands. If we moved, the kids would be close enough to walk to sporting events and ride their bikes to school. We could mail packages at the post office, buy our groceries, attend church, and go to a restaurant, all without getting in the car. In many ways, I thought downsizing our home and moving to Spruce Street would create a simpler life.

Living in town would have a lot of new experiences, but everything might not be so easy. If we moved, we wouldn't have an attached garage. I know that's something that a lot of people don't have, but I had gotten used to driving up to our two-car garage, pressing the automatic door opener on my visor, and pulling right into my spot. I never had to scrape ice off my windshield in the morning before work or carry a carload of groceries to the house in the pouring rain.

At the new house, we would have to park on the street. I was going to have to learn how to parallel park, something I avoided since I passed my driving test at sixteen. I was bad at it. If I had to park in town, I drove around, waiting for an empty spot at the beginning of a block that I could drive right into or I parked really far away. If Scott was riding with me, I made sure no one was behind us and put on my flashers to hop out of the car so that he could move to the driver's seat and park.

While I was excited that our new house would have a smaller yard to mow and take care of, I still intended to have a garden. I looked forward to planting the vegetables and herbs, watching them grow, and picking them when they were ripe. I loved looking at the lush green plants in their neat rows after I had weeded. For practically my whole life, I had lived by a field or an empty lot. As I worked in the garden, I filled up our wheelbarrow with weeds and clippings and then dumped it into the vacant area next to us. There would be no empty lot around our home on Spruce Street. I learned our town did have a program for residents to take branches and clippings to a site where it was turned into mulch, but the problem for us would be how to get it there. Neither our Prius or our minivan were ideal for hauling yard waste.

Things would be different for our kids as well. We had wide neighborhood streets where they rode their bikes. Almost everyone parked in their driveway or garage, and the few cars that passed by were usually neighbors who drove slowly, aware of the kids. No one used bike locks, and kids left their bikes in the yard or on the driveway. While none of these things were huge issues, they would mean changes for our family if we moved in town.

With our old house under contract, we didn't have to keep it neatly staged for buyers anymore. We could start packing and figuring out which pieces of furniture we could use in our new home.

We were living in a home that had 3,000 square feet with four bedrooms, an attached two-car garage, a large attic, and a full, dry basement. I had taken for granted all the storage: at least one large closet in each bedroom, along with a pantry, coat closet, linen closets, and laundry room shelves. Scott and I had a total of three closets in our bedroom, two with double folding doors in the bedroom and a spacious walk-in. It wasn't that we needed all the space we had, but we had grown accustomed to it.

The Spruce Street house had three bedrooms, some with small closets and others with nothing. There was no coat closet, pantry, or laundry room shelving. The basement occasionally got water, so we couldn't use it for storage until that problem was fixed. There was a detached garage in the alley behind us, but it was so small that I doubted even our Prius would fit. *Where were we going to put things?* It was like a huge jigsaw puzzle, there were so many pieces.

I was interested in the tiny living movement and liked reading about small living. One of the suggestions was to make furniture in a space do double duty. Choosing a hollow ottoman for our living room would provide a space inside to hold things and an extra seat. I was conscious about creating a functional space and increasing our storage.

Another concern for our family of five was that the house had only one shower. Very soon, we would have three teenagers, and everyone would be getting ready to leave in the mornings at the same time. We needed another full bathroom. The entire back section of the second floor had initially been one long, open room with no doors. We decided to divide it to create a bathroom for the kids and a bedroom with a closet for Natalie.

In our old house, she had the most furniture of anyone: a French Provincial bedroom suit that included a desk, dresser, makeup table, two nightstands, and framed mirrors. It was apparent that most of it wouldn't fit in the new room. There was only space in the room for her bed, a nightstand, and one other piece of furniture. With Natalie being an avid reader, it was more important to her to display her books than have a dresser. To accommodate the clothing, we planned extra shelves for her closet which would allow her to have a tall bookshelf in her room.

When her furniture set had been given to us, we knew it was good quality, but in bad shape. Scott and I spent a lot of time refinishing it and didn't want to break up the set. I hoped that someday, if Natalie had a daughter, she would pass the furniture on to her. Our attic had a nice staircase and tall ceilings, and I considered relocating some of the extra dressers up there to hold the kid's off-season clothes, beach towels, and other rarely used items.

Our current home had a sizable dining room, perfect for hosting the holidays. It was so big that when we first moved in, we had a table made to fit the room. We had selected a unique coffee colored stain and it took time to find the right pieces to match. When we found a Martha Stewart buffet and sideboard that matched perfectly, we had decided the quality craftsmanship was worth the price. Even if we took out the two leaves in the table, there was no room big enough to fit the table in our new house. We found a perfect space in the kitchen for our buffet, and the sideboard would fit in the family room to use it like an entertainment center.

Scott had arranged a schedule for the remodeling of our Spruce Street house. We hired contractors to complete some of the work so that we could finish and move in. We had been waiting to do a lot of it because we didn't have the money available. Now that our house would be selling, we would have money, but would be short on time to finish the house. Daily, we worked side by side with electricians, masons, HVAC techs, and plumbers.

One day, as I was in the bedroom pulling staples out of the trim, I looked out the window at the trees in full bloom. The view outside was unobstructed by curtains or blinds. I counted fourteen vehicles parked on our street, all there to help us finish our home. It was like an Amish barn raising and reminded me of when we built our very first house, which was also on a corner. My father-in-law, Jim, had nicknamed it "Pooh Corner." At the time, Scott and I were new college graduates, engaged to be married. We didn't have a lot of money, so we did as much of the work as we could to bring down the price. Friends and family members stopped by and we bought pizzas and beer for anyone who helped out. I remember how empowered I felt using a hammer for the first time, and how terrified I was to have a mortgage. We were on a time crunch when we built that house too. We wanted it completed for our wedding day, and we finished just in time.

This time our goal was to have Spruce Street finished before Natalie came home at the beginning of July. She had been against the move from the beginning. The house was in terrible condition when she left for France, and she wanted nothing to do with it. While she was gone, I tried to keep her involved in the process. I wanted her to be a part of our change. So, I explained how she would be next to a new bathroom, and I let her choose the paint colors and fixtures for her room. The mint green color she selected was now on the walls, and the pair of sparkly pendant lights she chose were installed.

One big project still remained: all the solid wood floors in the house needed to be sanded, stained, and polyurethaned. The settlement date for our old house was set for May 30th, but the floor refinishing wouldn't begin until June 6th. It would take two weeks to complete the floors, and we wouldn't be allowed access to the house during that time. We had been so focused on having the Spruce Street house ready for Natalie's return in July that we hadn't thought much about being out of our old house. Since there would be no way to move directly from our old house to our new house, we would have to move somewhere for two or three weeks until the house was finished. *Where were we going to live? Would we have to rent a storage unit for the contents of our whole home?*

We would have to move somewhere temporarily and find a place to store all our furniture. Then when our house was finished a few weeks later, we would have to move everything from our temporary housing and storage to our new house. In a matter of two or three weeks, we would be completely moving our household twice.

My mind quickly switched into solution mode, creating a plan to organize the logistics of the double move. We would need to separate our things into two groups: what we needed for the short-term and what could go into storage. If I could find any areas to stow things away at Spruce Street, I could save myself from moving stuff twice. The basement was out of the question because in the spring the basement had filled up with water. It was so deep that we stood in rain boots and used shovels to scoop water into buckets. Our detached garage was small, but it had a broken door that needed fixed. It was an old door and wouldn't be an easy repair. I realized that since our attic was unfinished, the floors there wouldn't be part of the refinishing project, so items up there would be protected.

Scott hadn't worked on the attic, since we weren't planning on finishing it for immediate living space. It wasn't insulated and once the weather turned warm, the heat from the roof made the room unbearable for more than a few minutes. It was one of the last places to get cleared out. I was intrigued with the attic and had gone up a few times. Walking up the steps was like stepping back in time. In the corner off to the right were stacks of newspapers chronicling the assassinations of President Kennedy and his brother, and the near melt down of Three Mile Island nuclear power plant, which was located in our town. I smelled the musty papers before I had even spotted them. There was a vintage bicycle and old model airplane kits. On the left side stood a beautiful wooden Victrola, a tall old-fashioned radio, and an antique television set.

With sweat dripping down my face, I looked around some more, and found a framed painting of our Spruce Street house propped up against a wall. It was taken in the spring with blooming pink azaleas surrounding the house. I could see how stunning it had looked when someone was caring for it. I didn't know if I would ever hang it up, but for the time being, I placed it aside as a piece to put on the mantle and evaluate more closely.

Although the attic was full, it was surprisingly organized. If I cleared it out, there would be a lot of room for storage.

I walked over to where the newspapers and magazines were and remembered the big black trunk that had been in that area when we took ownership of the house. The trunk annoyed me because it was right in the walkway. With full hands, I had tried unsuccessfully a few times to use my foot to move it to the side. Later, I put both hands on the long side and pushed with all my weight behind it, but it didn't budge—not even an inch.

One day, when I was tired of walking around it, I asked Scott to help me move it. I had no idea what was in it, and it was taking up valuable storage space.

"Can you help me move a trunk in the attic?"

He followed me up two floors to the attic, the heat rose with every step we climbed. He walked over and tried to push the chest out of the way, but nothing happened.

"What could be in here that it's so heavy it won't move at all?" He said.

"Maybe this is where they kept their money," I said wishfully. I had heard that sometimes people hid money in unusual places, so I said it every time Scott started to tear down a wall or we found an area we hadn't yet explored.

The trunk was locked. We had no idea where the key might have been, but I had a collection of keys I had found in the house. Some were unique skeleton keys for our antique doors and others looked like duplicate keys, but we probably had close to a hundred. I walked to the other side of the attic to look through some cardboard boxes, while Scott pulled tools out of his tool belt. The outside was not made of a very hard material. I heard him struggling as he tried to rip the case open with the claw end of a hammer and then I heard the loud sound of the material tearing.

"What in the world…?"

"Did you find money?" I asked.

"No, the trunk is screwed to the floor."

"Now it makes sense why neither of us could move it," I said.

"This is weird, there's a recording device in here and there are wires and extension cords coming out from the bottom of the trunk. This machine it hot, it's plugged in somewhere." Scott said.

He picked up the VCR to reveal a hole in the bottom of chest. After unscrewing the chest from the floor, he moved it to the side and saw the power cord went underneath a loose floor board. He followed it from the middle of the attic to the back. When he stopped, he was standing above the room that would be our boys' bedroom.

"The wires go in that closet, but I can't see inside," he said.

Just having a closet in the attic was out of the ordinary. I walked over to take a look. It was the size of a small bathroom. Up to this point, I had been too busy to work much in the attic. I peered inside, I saw heavy blankets and comforters hanging on a wooden rod that prevented us from seeing the back wall. Of course, like many of the places in this house, there was a switch—but no working lights. It was completely dark, so Scott went to get a flashlight.

When he returned to the attic, I reached for the flashlight to hold it for him, but he held on to it.

"I'm not going in. There could be a dead body back there," he said.

I should have been more afraid to go in, because as I had returned wedding photographs I found to people, they told me stories of how the previous owner had left their wedding early and never gave them pictures they had purchased. In clearing out the house, I had uncovered cardboard boxes full of paperwork showing that the previous owner was not an upstanding person. Documents detailed how he had used his power in positions of authority for personal gain and to take advantage of women.

"Someone has to go in," I said. As I pushed back the blankets, a small space with a sleeping bag was revealed. I unplugged the power cord from an outlet in the back wall.

"See, nothing to be afraid of," I teased as I dragged the sleeping bag out.

A few days later when Scott was removing old damaged plaster from the ceiling and walls of the boys' bedroom, directly below where the trunk had been in the attic, we were completely surprised to discover that the wires were connected to two pinhole cameras. I learned from women I talked to that the photographer had set up that room for the brides to change for their wedding announcement pictures that would be in the newspaper. The pinhole cameras filmed them as they were changing, I am sure, completely unaware. Scott added this new discovery to the list of items that creeped him out about the house. They included: the arson attempts and booby traps that were set by the previous owner's family and the piles of rags with an unknown substance on them in the master bathroom.

I had always felt that returning the wedding photographs was the right thing to do, but now I felt strongly that giving back the pictures somehow evened up the score for all the bad this person had put out into the world. Despite what had happened in the house, I still had hope living there would be a positive experience for my family. Just to be certain that no negative energy remained in the house, I made a mental note that I would sage the entire place, inside and out, before we moved in.

The next week, I went back up to work on squeezing more storage space out of the attic. As I looked around at all the things that needed to go, I decided to call a local antique store in the city. I made an appointment to show them the Victrola and other vintage pieces I had found. Even if I removed all the large things from the attic, there were still so many miscellaneous items to find homes for: ten boxes of rubber bands, dozens of small notepads, and nine new rolls of typewriter ribbon. Did anyone even use an electric typewriter anymore? Using Freecycle, I found homes for the dozens of three ring binders, so I listed the office supplies there. Ironically, the same woman who wanted the binders responded, saying her homeschool Co-op would love to take the rubber bands, notepads, and bags full of pens.

I was shocked when a different woman emailed about the typewriter ribbons. She said it was the exact ribbon she used. She was having a hard time finding them anymore and was thrilled. I had emailed her and didn't hear back, so I decided to call her to arrange for her to pick up the type writer ribbons. Not only did our conversation last longer than I expected, but I also felt like I got a blessing from the universe.

When Scott and I got home that night and started talking about our day, I remembered to tell him about the call. "I called a lady today who wanted the typewriter tape to give her our address, and you won't believe what happened."

"Is she coming to pick them up?"

"She was very excited about finding the type writer ribbon because she didn't think they made it anymore, and then told me she is a professional organizer. She focuses on moving. Can you believe it? What are the chances of that happening?"

"Have you ever met a professional organizer?"

"No. I told her I quit my job and started a business as a professional organizer. She asked if we had moved yet, and I told her we were just starting to pack. She said that she uses a color-coded system, and with the help of a few people on moving day, she can have a whole house unpacked, towels hung in the bathroom, and pictures on the wall the same day. Then she started explaining the system in detail as I took notes and asked questions for over half an hour."

"It sounds like you have a new project."

As I lay in bed that night, I thought about how I could have just emailed the lady our address for her to pick typewriter ribbons at our door and never actually spoken to her. Our conversation felt like divine intervention. I was definitely trying out the system for our move.

## *Color-Coded Move System*

- *Give each room in the new house a different color.*
- *Preplan where things will go in the new space, before you move in.*
- *Label the boxes with the color of the room the items will go into.*
- *Number the boxes.*
- *Use a notebook to list what you put into each box.*

# CHAPTER ELEVEN

# *Location, Location, Location*

Things you use regularly and value the most should be given highest priority and placed closest to where they are used.

Thankfully, Scott's parents offered to let us live with them until our house was ready. Jim and Diane had two huge garages where we could store all our furniture, so we didn't have to worry about renting a storage unit. They also didn't mind our cat, Piper. So, we planned to move in with them.

Since we would only be living there a few weeks, I had everyone pack their clothes in suitcases. With the contents of the rest of the house boxed, meticulously labeled and recorded in the "Move Notebook" I created. The weekend before our settlement, Scott and I rented a truck. We loaded and unloaded our stuff with Zach, Ryan, and Jim for two days until we were finally done on Sunday. My mind kept wandering to how much fun it would be to unpack and settle into our new house in a few short weeks. I was excited to test the moving system and see how fast we could get everything set up.

It had been a full year since I resigned from teaching, and while I didn't regret leaving, my organizing business had not taken off like I had hoped. I organized for my mom and some other friends, but besides them, I was working less than twenty hours a month. Now that we would be living with Scott's parents, I wouldn't have to worry about housework or keeping up with the yardwork. I would have more time to focus on getting clients.

I started with the fun task of choosing business cards. I wanted to find an image that would convey my passion for recycling. There were so many to choose from that I decided on a green background and a picture of the Earth.

The next task was the most crucial to my business; I had to find clients. The problem was that I wasn't exactly sure what to do. Advertising was completely foreign to me. As a teacher, I had never had to search for clients or promote myself; students just showed up in my room.

Since I really didn't have any money, I planned to use word of mouth to get started. I found a new networking group made up of businesses that focused on health and well-being. It sounded like the perfect setting to introduce my business, Healthier Spaces Organizing. I knew from the clients I had worked with that decluttering their homes made them breathe easier and reduced their overall stress levels. When I donated the excess items to charities and recycled instead of putting things in landfills, I was keeping Mother Earth healthy.

At most networking events, everyone does a thirty-second commercial explaining their business to the group. I wrote out what I wanted to say and practiced it several times until I knew it by heart. When I arrived at the restaurant with my brand-new business cards in hand, forty people were already gathered at small tables. Some had gotten lunch and were eating while they waited for the leader to welcome the group. I didn't have money to spend on lunch, but if I did, I don't think I could have eaten anything that day with the butterflies in my stomach.

Suddenly, I felt like I was a 9th grader back in speech class instead of commanding the room like the teacher I had been for the last eighteen years. For so long, I had been so afraid of failing and being ridiculed about my business that I hadn't talked about it much. This would be the first time I would be introducing my new career to a room full of people, putting myself out there. *What if they didn't take me seriously?*

Going in order, one at a time, people stood up and did their commercial. There were yoga instructors, health coaches, and people who sold supplements, but I could hardly focus on what they were saying. I was rehearsing what I would say while counting the number of people before my turn.

When my turn finally came, I stood up and faced the group. I introduced myself and noticed a look of interest on their faces as I told them I was a professional organizer. People smiled and nodded as I spoke. One person shouted out, "I could use you!" I felt relieved when I sat back down.

I was certain that after people heard about my service and saw how passionate I was about organizing and saving the environment, they would become instant clients. I imagined they would probably come up at the end and ask for my card for someone they knew, and my calendar would quickly fill up. When the meeting ended and no one had scheduled a session, I kept a positive attitude and told myself that they probably just needed to think about what I said and would call tomorrow.

The next day, I kept my cell phone close by, sure that it would ring, and I would book more organizing sessions. I was so disappointed when no one called. Getting clients was going to be harder than I imagined. *What did I do wrong?*

I shared my experience about the networking group with a friend who owned her own business. She suggested that at the next networking event, I offer a discounted session to the people in the room. Then I would get some instant clients, work out some of the kinks of running a business, and start making money. I was definitely not as nervous at the next networking function, and I was eager to try the new strategy.

Offering a special rate worked. I was thrilled to schedule three organizing sessions on my calendar. The first one was a week away. With excitement, I counted down the days until our session. We would be organizing my new client's kitchen.

During the drive to her house later that week, my mind was racing. *What if I get there and don't know what to do? What if when we are finished, she doesn't think it's good enough?*

As my client opened the door, I was surprised to see she looked troubled.

"I am so overwhelmed that I don't even know where to start," she said.

I had been to her house once before for a consultation, so it wasn't the first time I was seeing her space. The countertops were full of appliances and food that didn't fit into the already packed cupboards. There was no space left to prepare food. Immediately, I knew we should start emptying the cabinets and getting rid of expired food and any kitchen items she didn't use. This would create the room in the cabinets for the things on the counter.

After a few minutes, I heard my client sigh.

"What's going on?" I asked.

"I don't know what I should do with this platter."

"Do you use it?"

"No, but it was a gift from a friend. I want to keep it, but I don't know where."

"We could put the platter in the cabinet above the refrigerator. It's a hard to reach space, and that way you can save the closer cabinets for things you use regularly."

She seemed happy with that option, and I continued asking her questions and offering suggestions throughout the session. I realized my active listening helped her make decisions and clarify her vision for the space. At the end of our time, my client said she was tired but very happy with the changes.

I drove home feeling content and proud of my work. As I started organizing for other clients, they all expressed gratitude for my help, each in their own way. Many hugged me and said they felt like they could breathe again, they felt free and alive. I could relate to how they were feeling. When I had been teaching, I had a stagnant, stifled feeling and now I felt fully conscious. One client greeted me in her driveway with a huge smile, calling out, "It's happy hour!" when I drove up for our session. My heart swelled each time a client emailed me thanking me for helping them to reclaim their spaces.

I wanted to spend every day organizing, but I didn't have enough clients yet. I had made a deal with myself: if I didn't have an organizing session scheduled, I had to try to pick up a waitressing shift. I dreaded going back to that toxic environment.

There was a big divide between the full- and part-time servers. The regular staff talked loudly about the way "certain people" did this or that, referring to myself and the other occasional workers. We tried to stay to ourselves and talked quietly to each other. I told some of my coworkers about the house we bought and my organizing business. When we worked together, they asked for updates. They were eager to hear about my successes and rooted for me to follow my dream.

Other servers overhead and spitefully said, "I guess it isn't going that well if you're still working here."

They were right. My business had started growing, but slowly. I definitely still needed to waitress. As I got dressed to work a banquet, I tried to put on the attitude that their comments didn't bother me, but they did. I wasn't used to people constantly watching me, waiting and hoping I would make a mistake so that they could pounce on me. It was stressful. I don't have thick skin, but I couldn't let them know they got to me.

As the evening went on, we had finished serving dinner and dessert for a wedding reception. The servers could stay in the kitchen area until the festivities came to an end, and it was time to clean up. Trying to steer clear of the negative comments of the staff, I asked the manager if I could go into the ballroom. He didn't mind, so I stood against the wall watching the bridal party dancing, feeling excitement in the air.

I thought back to my wedding day. I remembered being too excited the day of our wedding and throughout the entire reception to eat. By the time we reached our hotel, I was starving. We had used a credit card to pay for our overnight stay and planned to charge the meals to the room, so we didn't bring our wallets. We were going to treat ourselves with room service. When we called to place our order, we found out the kitchen was closed. It was our honeymoon night, and we were starving and hadn't brought money. Then we remembered the money from our dollar dance.

It was a tradition in my family for guests to give a dollar (or a few) to dance with the bride or groom. My mom insisted it was a good way for our invited guests to have a private moment to wish us well and send us along with a little extra money. Our friends and relatives twisted and folded the bills like they were making origami.

It took us a few minutes to straighten a handful of dollars, and Scott went into the hallway to buy a handful of snacks from the vending machine. We laughed at our situation as we sat on the bed, inhaling our chips and cookies for our first meal together as a married couple.

While waitressing, I especially loved being in the room during weddings, but I tried to stay in the room during any event. Typically, I was the only staff member to stay in the room, but I took any opportunity I could to escape being under the watchful eyes of the staff.

I was pressed up against the wall in the back of a large room when a celebrity "housewife" came to speak. The room was packed with tables of women enjoying their specialty meal. I stood listening to her talking about her life and giving an inspiring message to the crowd. From the time I started working there, my goal had been to make my organizing business successful enough that I didn't have to waitress again. Now, I imagined what it would be like if I were the one speaking at the podium with several hundred people in the audience. I had no idea what I would be speaking about, but it became a new goal of mine.

---

### *Deciding what to do with an item?*

### *Ask yourself the following questions:*

- *Do I need it?*
- *Do I use it?*
- *Do I love it?*

*If it doesn't check one of these boxes, chances are you should move it out of your life.*

---

# CHAPTER TWELVE

# *Live in the Present*

When discarding items, don't get too caught up in keeping everything from the past or worrying too much about what you "could" use in the future.

When you get on a plane and the flight attendants are going over the routine safety information, they instruct you to put on your own oxygen mask first, if the situation arises, and then help children and others who need assistance. In my late thirties, I started to realize I had unconsciously been putting everyone else first. I was running out of oxygen.

It initially began when I had children, as the biological response to meet their needs, until they were old enough to take care of themselves. Slowly, like so many mothers, I set aside my needs and ambitions for that of the family. As the years went by, it became difficult to remember who I was and what my hopes and dreams were.

I had to reconnect to myself and learn who I had become as an adult. Acupuncture sessions became a sacred time where I could quiet my mind and tune in.

Since I had started the treatments for medical reasons, I hadn't expected the ancient practice to have such an impact on my mental clarity. Each time I drove to see my acupuncturist, Becky, my head was full of lists. Things that needed to be done, groceries to buy, and people to contact. I would sit in the parking lot, texting and making phone calls until the time of my appointment. I rushed into the waiting room and sat down on the brown overstuffed couch that seemed to swallow me up. As I sat with my phone turned off, I noticed my breathing started to slow down.

During my sessions, I described physical symptoms and concerns to Becky. She was able to bridge the connection between my experiences and the impact they had on my body. As she inserted the needles, I felt a pulsing release when they hit the right spot. I closed my eyes and listened to the rhythmic beating of drums that played from a CD and fell into a twilight sleep. When I woke up, my mind was clear, and I felt refreshed. I walked outside at a slower, more mindful pace.

I sat in my car and watched the river for a few minutes. In the winter, it was white and full of sharp, slow moving shards of ice. During warmer months, the river was a deep blue, and the water moved swiftly. I started the engine and turned off the radio. My priorities changed, and the items on my to do lists no longer seemed urgent.

Daily life clutters our mind and spirit. These treatments brought me back to the space where I could become aware of my life. I thought about what was important to me. Trying to live more consciously, I wouldn't schedule anything else on acupuncture days. I wanted to preserve this feeling as long as I could.

As the school year came to an end and summer vacation started, finishing our home was on the top of our priority list. Scott left his parent's house early each morning and headed to Spruce Street. Some days, I followed him in my car, wearing my jeans with the worn-out knees and paint all over them.

The sun was just starting to rise, and the air was cool and still. It seemed like the whole town was asleep as Scott pulled folding chairs out to the front porch, and we sat and drank coffee. These were the only moments we were completely alone. Our days were so long and busy that I yearned for the few calm minutes we spent together

Each day when we were too exhausted to do anymore work, we went back to Jim and Diane's house to eat dinner and spend some time with the boys. We were bone tired from all the physical work. As gross as I was, if Scott would have let me, I would have fallen into bed, without even showering.

On the days when I didn't work at the house, I said goodbye to the boys and my in-laws in my black-and-white clothing. I usually waitressed two to four times a week and shifts often went late into the night. I had been there for several months, so I knew the routine. I did my job and didn't waste time trying to win over callous coworkers. While I couldn't ignore all their snide comments, I reminded myself I wouldn't be working there forever. Instead, I used the time to focus on ways I could improve my business.

There was terrible reception in the building, so I was in the habit of checking my phone once I got into my car and locked the doors. I scrolled through the messages and missed calls. That night, I noticed the guy we were hiring to refinish our wood floors had called. I would call him in the morning since it was after midnight. On the drive home, I counted the hours I worked and figured out how much money I would have in my next paycheck. I was grateful for the income but prayed daily that I wouldn't need to go back.

I called Scott. He would be wondering when I was coming home.

"I'm on my way home. How was your night?" I asked.

"Fine, my mom made London Broil on the grill. Zach and Ryan loved it, and, of course, then they each had big bowls of party cake ice cream. How was your night?"

It was such a blessing to be living with Jim and Diane as we were trying to finish the house. They watched the boys while we worked during the day and cooked dinner for all of us at night. Typical of grandparents, they loved to indulge Zach and Ryan with their favorite junk foods.

"Work was OK," I said. Scott had so much going on at the new house. He didn't need to be burdened with hearing that I despised the only secure job we had.

"OK. I'll probably be asleep when you get home. Good night," he said.

When I walked in, the house was quiet. My neck and left shoulder ached from carrying heavy trays full of dishes, and my feet throbbed from hours of standing. I showered quickly and crawled into bed.

My body was tired, but I had a hard time winding down when I worked late. As I lay in bed, I jumped a little as I remembered a guest earlier in the evening who had asked for a cup of hot tea. *I forgot to take tea to that lady.*

I tossed and turned thinking about my schedule for the week. In the morning, I was speaking to a women's church group about downsizing.

I woke up early to make phone calls, check on the delivery of our appliances and a special order front door, and research items to sell on eBay. When I looked at my phone, I was reminded about the missed call from the man refinishing our floors. He would be starting in a few days. I wondered what he wanted as I dialed his number.

"Sorry I didn't call back yesterday. It was too late when I saw your call."

He said, "I was calling to give you a more realistic timeframe of when I can start your floors."

I was confused. "What do you mean '*a more realistic timeframe*'? We have you scheduled to begin sanding the floors next week on the 6th."

He said, "I'm not going to be able to start until the 22nd."

My mind raced as I flipped through my day planner, searching for the 22nd. It was a Sunday and two weeks later than he was supposed to start. That would push all the other projects back—we would be behind schedule.

I started to panic. "Let me get this straight. You are going to start on Sunday the 22nd of *June*?"

He answered, "No, the 22nd of *July*."

*Oh, no. Oh, no. This can't be happening.*

It would take two weeks to finish the floors, and during that time, no one could be working in the house. We would have to reschedule the contractors and other work that was waiting for the floors to be done. So, at the earliest, we wouldn't move into the house until late August. In one phone call, our whole remodeling schedule had crumbled.

My heart sank, and tears flooded my eyes as I thought how we told Natalie our home would be ready when she returned next month. The transition from France was going to be difficult. I wanted everything to be perfect for her return. Now she would have to move into Scott's parents' house with us and then move again. *Where could she even go?* There weren't any empty bedrooms. We already had Zach and Ryan sharing a small room with one of them sleeping on the hardwood floor.

*What if the floor sander didn't start on the new date he gave us?*

I dreaded telling Scott. He was working so hard to get everything finished.

I had to push the upsetting news about the floors to the back of my mind and get ready to speak to the women's group. As I drove to the banquet facility, I rehearsed my presentation. I arrived early so that I could find the host and set up a display of before-and-after organizing pictures. I looked at the programs laid out at each seat and learned I would be speaking to the group after the meal. The forty women slowly trickled into the room for the monthly luncheon.

I had decided to focus my talk on downsizing since most of the attendees were retired. I knew that my own grandparents struggled with getting rid of their possessions when the time came to downsize. The main reason they had trouble discarding their belongings was because they didn't want to be wasteful. They had grown up during the Great Depression, when saving and conserving resources was ingrained in them. As newlyweds, my relatives had nothing and were so grateful for any donations they were given. Now, they wanted to help their children and grandchildren the same way. The problem was that my parents and I didn't have the room for their things.

I explained to the group of ladies that younger generations tended to favor a more minimalist decorating style. Current brides-to-be no longer registered for a china pattern or crystal and most have no need for a china cabinet. I encouraged them to ask their family before holding on to anything for them. I could understand that they wanted their things to be appreciated. I offered the option of donating to a charity so that someone could benefit from the things they no longer needed. Often, we may not know the person who needs our things the most. In the end, isn't it less wasteful to donate our unwanted items, rather than have them go unused?

Afterwards, some of the women came up to talk and thanked me for the information that gave them a lot to discuss with their families. They said I was a good speaker and "looked comfortable in front of a crowd." It made me smile. I had a lot of practice talking in front of a group. I was still using my teaching skills, just with a more mature audience.

As I walked to my car, I remembered about the hardwood floors. I went to my in-laws' house to change into my construction work clothes before going to the Spruce Street house. I had to go talk to Scott.

When I pulled up to our Spruce Street home with my windows down, I could hear the classic rock music station playing on the large yellow and black DeWalt battery charger radio. There were fewer people in the house as we were getting closer to being finished. I was glad Scott was alone as I told him about the phone call with the floor refinisher.

He was furious. "Find another refinisher."

We had been working on the house for a full year and were down to the final stretch. The boys were getting restless living at their grandparents' house. Running back and forth between Spruce Street and Jim and Diane's was wearing Scott and I down.

I started making phone calls right away. Each contractor told me they couldn't come out for two–three months, and that was only for an initial consultation. I left messages for others and hoped they would call back with more availability, but it looked like we would have to take our chances with the first guy. I was crushed.

When I was hired to organize an office the next week, I was happy to have something to take my mind off our house situation. I had organized a few home offices, but this was the first completely separate office that also had employees. I wondered if I was ready to take on a business this size.

My client discussed concerns of the space with me, and one of the problems was organizing shared supplies. Time and money were wasted looking for things. I realized I could apply the same principles I used when organizing in a kitchen. The frequency of use and location of items were key to creating a functional and efficient work space. I set up a system where each shelf had a theme, and similar items were placed together. This made it easy to find things like when you shop in an office supply store. It also made taking inventory more efficient.

As we organized the space, my client told me about renovations he was doing on a new property he had purchased. His project was much larger than ours, but I was so interested in hearing about it because our jobs were on similar timelines. When I shared with him the problems we were having with getting our floor refinished, he gave me the name of a reputable person his fiancée had used.

As soon as our organizing session ended, I called the number. I was optimistic when the man said he could come for a consultation in a few days.

It upset me that there was no way we could finish the house before Natalie came home, but as I thought about how everything was getting pushed back, I realized we had a bigger problem.

Now, we were down to less than two months until fall sports practices started. Once football started, Scott wouldn't have any time to work on the house. If we didn't finish the house in the next couple of weeks, we wouldn't be able to move out of his parents' house until Christmas.

**Reasons people have a hard time getting rid of things, and ideas to combat them:**

- ***I may need it someday.*** *Will it still be good by the time you need it? Will you remember where you stored it? Is it something you could repurchase easily for less than $10 if you do need it? If so, then I say take the risk. It won't cost you much if you do need to buy it again.*

- ***It's good stuff. Someone could use it.*** *You are right. Someone could use it! Offer the items you don't need to family and friends first and then to charities. It feels great to know someone else will love and use your things.*

- ***I want to preserve the memories.*** *There are many ways to preserve memories without keeping the actual items. Take a picture of your keepsakes and write down the story about why it is so special to you. A book detailing all your family memories would be a wonderful gift to give to relatives.*

- ***I don't know where to start.*** *If you start in a space you don't use often, you are likely to uncover things you haven't seen in quite a while. It will probably be easier to let go of these items.*

# CHAPTER THIRTEEN

# *Spend Time in Your Space*

Take time to use and enjoy the space you have
created.

We had not seen Natalie in nearly ten months. It had been a difficult year for us to have our sixteen-year-old daughter living so far away from home. My heart ached so badly when she left for France that I cried for a week. A six-hour time difference made it hard to connect with her. I missed talking to her and knowing what was going on in her daily life. We planned Skype sessions, but often, they ended in frustration when the computer screen froze up.

I requested to waitress on all the holidays, because I knew they would be emotionally difficult for me. If I was working, then it wouldn't really feel like a special day and maybe I wouldn't miss Natalie so much. It wasn't until I was out shopping one day that it really hit me-Natalie wouldn't be with us for Christmas. I was so upset, I decided to leave the store and go home. On my way out, I ran into a neighbor who asked how my "babies" were doing. I immediately burst into tears. At that time, I wasn't going to see Natalie for another six months.

From the day she left, I counted the months until she would be home. Now, it was less than a month. At the end of the exchange program, Natalie was finishing her school year, saying goodbye to all the new friends she had met and trying to figure out how to fit all her clothes and souvenirs into her suitcase.

We barely talked because she wanted to spend the last weeks soaking in as much of the experience as she could. She knew that we had sold our house and moved in with her grandparents, but we didn't mention anything about the floors being delayed and how that had pushed back the other contractors. She never asked where we would be living when she came home, and we didn't bring it up. I thought it would be better to tell her in person.

The only space left in Scott's parents' house was a small room, like a nursery, inside their master bedroom. Diane and I wanted to make it as comfortable as we could for Natalie. We moved a bed and dresser into the space. As we put on the yellow sheets and a new comforter, it reminded me of decorating her nursery. I thought how I anxiously anticipated her arrival for the first time seventeen years before. I wanted everything to be just right. Maybe then she wouldn't mind as much if she had to stay in this room for a while.

Natalie and all the other students who had gone on a study abroad in Europe were arriving at the JFK airport in New York. It was a three-hour drive from where we lived. I was overcome with emotion every time I thought about seeing her.

Zach and Ryan were not excited about spending the whole day in the car and an airport. For the last month, Scott and I had been working long hours at the house. We hadn't done anything as a family in weeks, so we decided to make the best of the drive and plan some fun stops along the way.

We left early in the morning and played an alphabet game, searching for road signs that started with each letter of the alphabet. Letter Q was always a tough one to find.

Zach, a geography wiz, commented, "Too bad there aren't signs inviting people to vacation in the Middle Eastern country of Qatar, then we could find a Q."

Ryan groaned, he hated when Zach tried to teach him something.

"You should learn about these places, Ryan." Zach continued.

Ryan shrugged his shoulders and smirked as he said, "It doesn't care."

The awkward phrase set Zach off. "It's '*I don't care*' or '*It doesn't matter*,' NOT '*It doesn't care*'"

And with that, they were bickering away.

It reminded me of a few years earlier when we decided that instead of having things to open for Christmas, our gift to the kids would be an experience. We bought tickets to see Rutgers play in a bowl game in Florida. It was too expensive to fly there, so we decided to drive the twenty plus hours with all five of us in the Prius. There was a lot of arguing on that journey, but we had made so many great memories. This trip would be much shorter. After an hour, we stopped for breakfast.

We were talking with the boys and waiting for our food when my phone buzzed.

"Is everything OK?" Scott asked.

"It's a text from a mother whose son is on the same flight as Natalie. She said their first plane left

France on time. They should arrive around four," I said, tears running down my cheek.

"Are you crying? What's wrong, Mom?" Ryan asked.

"Mom is just really excited to see Natalie," Scott said.

We had several hours to occupy, so we made a detour to Scott's alma mater, Rutgers University. The stop gave the boys a chance to get out of the car and burn off some energy. Scott showed them the stadium and practice fields where he played football.

As we walked around the school bookstore, letting the boys each pick out a t-shirt, my phone buzzed again. I was afraid to look at the screen. I was so worried the flight would be delayed and it would be even longer until we were reunited with Natalie. Thankfully, the text from the same woman informed me that our children's second flight left on time. I wanted to get to the airport. I didn't care if we had to sit there for hours and wait for her. *What if we hit traffic?*

We walked into the airport and saw all the families anxiously waiting for their children who had gone abroad for the year. Each one held bunches of balloons, flowers, and signs for their child. We took our place beside them, Zach and Ryan raising the posters they made for Natalie. I think Ryan copied Zach's idea, but each one had a French flag and an American flag and said, "Bonjour! Welcome Home, Natalie."

"When is she going to be here?" Zach asked.

"Do I have to keep holding up my sign?" Ryan complained.

We all kept looking down the corridor, impatient for the first glimpse of her. When I spotted Natalie, my eyes instantly flooded with tears. I watched as she talked to friends. She looked different, more mature. I couldn't wait. I wanted to run to her. It seemed like it took forever for her to make her way down to us. I hugged her tightly, and I didn't want to let her go.

We quickly gathered her bags and hurried out of the airport to our car. I wanted to hear all about her experience, but Natalie sat in the back seat of the car with the boys who were busy catching up with their sister.

Ryan started, "Say something in French."

"What do you want me to say?" she asked.

"I don't care. I just want to hear what it sounds like."

"Qu'est-ce que tu veux que je te dise?"

I was amazed at her accent. Even though I had taken four years of French in high school, when she spoke, I had no idea what she was saying.

"What did you say?" Ryan asked.

"I said, 'What do you want me to tell you?'"

Zach wanted to know about the political parties in France and what she learned in school about the Holocaust. Ryan wasn't interested in hearing about the French government; he just wanted to be close to Natalie.

My heart was full as I listened to them talk. I was so happy to have everyone together again. I wanted to prolong our time in the car as long as I could. So, we took our time driving and stopped for sushi. I wanted to shut out the rest of the world and put my little family in a bubble. Natalie was home with us again, and I wasn't ready to share her just yet.

For the first few days at Jim and Diane's, Natalie caught up on her sleep and visited with her friends. I thought she would like to see her new room, but she didn't ask at all about the Spruce Street house.

"Let's go see the house today," I said over breakfast.

"Do I *have* to?" she asked.

The boys hadn't been there in a while either. Scott and I decided to take all the kids. We wanted to show off all the work we had done.

From the street, major changes were evident. In the last year, we had removed the overgrown bushes, broken sidewalk, broken brick pond structure, and the ratty green outdoor carpeting.

We walked in through the new front door to the open kitchen area. Everything was sparkling and new: white cabinets, black quartz countertops, and stainless-steel appliances. The previously disastrous master bathroom with the broken tile floor and the orange sheet that covered the toilet was transformed. It looked chic with new grey subway tile and a shiny silver chandelier hanging over a vintage royal blue clawfoot tub. When we showed Natalie her room, I hoped she would fall in love with it, but she looked disinterested.

As we walked through the house, it was difficult for me to remember the stained carpet that was once there as the bare wood floors lay waiting to be refinished. It was like we had blended modern conveniences with the charm of our old home. Our house looked beautiful.

The kids continued to call our house "The Dump," but it no longer looked or smelled like it did when we bought it. We had built a brand-new house inside of the original house. We joked that the only thing we kept were the bricks on the inside.

"We have been working on this house every day for months. We have done too much work for you to call it *The Dump*," Scott said, angry that they were not more appreciative of our efforts. That was the last time the kids referred to our house that way.

There were still a lot of little projects that needed to be finished, but the floors were first. When the refinisher met us at the house, it was easy to see he was knowledgeable about hardwood floors. I thought I would hug him when he said he would start the floors the next week and finish them in ten days. Our summer routine of working long hours every day would be on hold. While the floors were being sanded and stained, we wouldn't be able to be in the house. It would be a well-needed break. The boys were starting to pick at each other after two months of not having their own space, and we wanted to spend time reconnecting as a family with Natalie.

We decided to take the kids into town for some entertainment. Scott and I had both wanted to live in town when we were their age. There were so many places they could walk to and things they could do. The first night, we walked to an ice cream shop a few blocks away from our new house. The sun was going down, so we sat outside at a picnic table eating our cones and talking. We told the kids about the parks that were down the street and an old-time movie theater. We wanted them to share our excitement about moving there.

Each July, our church had a four-day festival with games, small rides, and carnival food. Natalie wasn't interested in it anymore, but Zach and Ryan still loved going. It was only two blocks away from our new house, so the next night, for the first time, we let them meet up with some friends and go by themselves.

Scott and I took folding chairs from the front porch around to our backyard. We got a bottle of wine and glasses from the local dollar store and sat under the stars.

In the distance, the sound of the rides and games became quieter as the night went on. Then we heard the boys talking and laughing as they walked up to the house. They excitedly told us about the games they played and showed us goldfish they won. I wasn't thrilled about having to take care of the fish, but I was happy to see them having fun at our new house. Maybe they would like living here after all.

The floors were finished in the promised time, and the essential plumbing and electrical projects resumed. When we moved into Jim and Diane's house, each with our suitcase of clothes, we planned on being there for two or three weeks. That was nearly three months earlier. It was time for Ryan's football practices to start, and we had to find his helmet and shoulder pads that were stored away in the garage. Those weren't the only things we needed though. Natalie's entire room had been packed up for the move, and she had a lot of things she wanted to find. It was my chance to try out the color-coded packing system. As I had placed items into boxes, I recorded each one in my note book.

I designated a different color for every room in our new house. Anything to go in Ryan's room was labeled with a green marker, things for Natalie's room were labeled with a purple marker, and the kitchen was orange. To find Ryan's football gear, I just found the green section in my notebook along with the box and number that contained his football gear. We could pinpoint the exact box we needed and not have to rummage through everything. It was a good thing I had packed this way because if we stayed much longer, we would soon have to find the kids' fall school clothes.

The color-coded packing system seemed like a service I could offer to my clients who were moving. During the winter, when we had put our renovations on hold, I wanted to read and learn everything I could about organizing. There were so many books and magazines with interesting suggestions for storing household items and maximizing spaces. Although I liked seeing innovative ways to store things, I really felt that most people needed help letting go of their stuff, not just finding a pretty container to put it in.

I discovered my favorite organizing guru, Peter Walsh, when he was a guest on the Oprah show. When I read his book *Does This Clutter Make My Butt Look Fat?* I realized that my philosophy of organizing most closely resembled his. His style focused on purging and getting rid of the things you didn't need anymore. He wrote about how clutter holds people back and weighs them down, making them feel exhausted and overwhelmed. The effects of the clutter aren't contained in a room; they often spill outside of the closet doors into other areas of our lives.

When I started organizing with new clients, I asked their goal for the space. Often the answer would be "I just want it organized." I saw *The Life-Changing Magic of Tidying Up* by Marie Kondo and other books about organization on their shelves. They were trying to figure out how to fit their lives into a system. Everyone is unique, and they weren't able to apply the information to their situation.

I think people often lack a vision of what it is they want to create, and it is important to help them define their goals. Saying you want to be "organized" sounds a lot like when people go on a diet and say they want to "lose weight." How will you know when you've met your goal? Some people feel their small appliances should have a home in plain sight, not hidden away in a cabinet. Other people think a kitchen feels organized when there is nothing on the countertops, not even a coffee maker or toaster.

The first sessions with a new client weren't always easy. I'm a stranger in their home, and they're exposing their lives to me. I knew they felt vulnerable. Some anticipate our organizing session with feelings of dread. I imagine they feel like I do when I visit my dentist. He is a family friend whom I enjoy talking to, but I hate going to my biannual appointments. I am fearful each time as I wait to be called back to the chair. I have even said to him and his staff, "It's not you; it's me." I am grateful that he's good at his job and relieved when we're done.

I knew my clients would feel more at ease once they were involved and could see change taking place, so I helped them get started right away with something easy. Once the session was underway and they were busy, they seemed to relax a little more. Often, I am so eager to begin organizing, just like when I cleared out our Spruce Street kitchen the first night, that I forget to take pictures first. My excitement and energy continue through the session.

It feels so good to be fully engaged in my job. Clients comment, "You really *like* doing this, don't you?" To have the passion for my job so evident to the people I work for, made me feel blessed to have found my purpose.

## *Purging is not something you do once and never need to do again.*

*Things are constantly entering your home and life, and you must evaluate whether you want them to stay. Making rules will help you maintain your space. Below are some suggestions.*

- *After you wear a piece of clothing that was hanging in your closet, turn the hanger the other direction. At the end of the season, review all the hangers that were not turned. Since you didn't wear them, maybe it's time to donate them.*

- *If you have magazines piling up, cancel your subscriptions until you can catch up.*

- *For each new item you bring into your home, think about donating an item.*

- *Not sure if you are ready to get rid of something? Put an "expiration date" on it. Plan to check it again in a month or two to see if you can let it go.*

- *Look at your calendar. Are you happy with how you are spending your time? Is there something you could cut out?*

# CHAPTER FOURTEEN

# *Finish One Space*

Stick with a room until you are done.
It is motivating to see the completed space. Each area
you finish makes it easier to do the next space
because you have made decisions about what will
and will not go into a room.

Our end of summer practice schedule was in full swing: Natalie had tennis practice, Zach and Ryan each had football practice, and Scott was coaching high school football. This year, each person's sport was at a different location and time.

Since we had moved in with his parents, Scott had been leaving their house about 6:30 am and not returning until around 8:00 pm. However, instead of working on the house, he was at football.

There wasn't a lot we needed to finish at Spruce Street. We decided certain projects like installing the baseboard trim and final painting were tabled until after we moved in. Natalie started asking every day when we were moving into our house. It wasn't that she was that excited to go to the new house, but she just wanted her own room to unpack and get settled. We explained that we needed to have an occupancy permit before we were allowed to move in. The code enforcement officer, the person responsible for issuing the permit, had a full schedule, and it would be another week until he could fit us in. The inspection was scheduled for August 12th, our wedding anniversary.

The night of August 11th, Scott came back to his parents exhausted from coaching all day and went to bed shortly after eating. I could hardly sleep. I tossed and turned, praying the inspector would not find any reason to deny our permit.

When I woke up on August 12th, it was early, but Scott had already left for practice. We didn't have a scheduled time to meet the inspector, but he would call on his way to our house. I planned to call Scott so that he could leave football practice and be there to answer any questions.

I walked into the kitchen for breakfast, and I was surprised to see Natalie sitting in her pajamas with Diane. She told me her morning tennis practice was canceled because of the rain. I looked out the sliding glass doors, and it wasn't just raining—it was pouring. I had volunteered to help serve the football team lunch, and since they still practiced in the rain, I put on jeans and pulled on my brown and pink polka dot rain boots.

I arrived in the cafeteria to start setting up at 10:00 am. It required a lot of people to feed the fifty players and ten coaches. A crew of parents, grandparents, and supporters volunteered to serve lunch and then clean up afterward. I stood in the serving line giving a scoop of pasta to each person. The coaches were the last in line, and as they passed they said "Happy anniversary" to me. Scott must have told them. I was so worried about the inspector coming that I had completely forgotten.

Everyone was sitting at the cafeteria tables eating when my cell phone rang. It was the inspector. He was already at our house and waiting for us. I ran over to the table of coaches to tell Scott. We rushed out the door, hurrying to the parking lot to find Scott's truck. I was so worried that the inspector would leave before we could drive the two miles to our house.

When we got there, I didn't wait until Scott parked before I jumped out of the truck to meet the inspector who was already on our porch. He wrote notes on his clipboard as he walked through the house with Scott. I stood in the kitchen, my stomach in knots.

When he was done, he explained two small concerns he had about outlets and said he could come back to check them. I was so relieved when he signed the permit and said we could move in.

As the inspector closed the door, I turned to Scott and said, "Aren't you excited? We can move in now!"

He said, "We can't move in today. It's pouring outside. Everything would get soaked. Plus, I have football practice tonight. We'll have to wait. Maybe this weekend."

I was crushed. We had never discussed moving that day. I just had it in my mind that we would move as soon as we got the OK. I was so concerned about getting the permit that I hadn't even thought about the weather or how we would get everything to the new house.

Scott kissed me and said, "Happy anniversary," and hurried out the door to practice. I locked up the house and drove back to the school to finish cleaning up the cafeteria. I felt so sad as I wheeled large containers of pasta and coolers full of

Powerade to the walk-in fridge. We finally had a permit, but we still couldn't move. Rain was ruining the day.

When I walked into Jim and Diane's, everyone wanted to know how the inspection went. Natalie got a huge smile on her face when I said we had an occupancy permit.

"I'll go get my stuff. Zach and Ryan…go pack your clothes!" she yelled as she started running up the stairs to get her things.

"Natalie, we can't move today. It's raining too hard. There aren't any beds at the new house, and I'm sure we can't fit a mattress in the Prius."

She sulked and flopped down on the couch as I went to start a load of laundry.

Our friends from the old neighborhood called to ask Zach and Ryan to come over to hang out. I was happy to drop them off for a little while and have them burn off some energy with their friends.

When I walked back in the house, Natalie started talking before I even walked through the door. "The rain stopped, Mom. Can we move in now?"

She was right; it wasn't raining at all. We still had a problem though. How were we going to move all of our stuff? When we moved things into the garages, we had rented a moving truck. I didn't want to waste time renting a truck. There had to be someone with a pickup truck. I remembered Les had one. Maybe I could borrow that?

It was 4:00 pm when Natalie and I picked up my sister's truck and started wiping the water out of the back. The two of us were on a mission: we were going to sleep at our new house that night. We divvied up the work, quickly stripping all the beds and putting the sheets, blankets, and pillows inside the truck. She packed suitcases of clothing for her and the boys while I did the same for Scott and me. We felt empowered as we loaded the boys' twin mattresses into the truck and unloaded them at our new house. All we needed to do was move her bed and mine.

Scott's parents were shocked that we had decided to move that day.

Jim warned, "I was watching the weather, and the rain isn't over. You guys should probably stop moving things. No one decides to move mattresses in a rainstorm."

We hadn't planned to move. But it wasn't raining anymore, and we were almost done. Natalie's full mattress went in easily, but my queen-size mattress was too heavy and wide for the two of us to lift. In a hurry, we decided to take her mattress since it was already in the truck. I would have Scott help me bring our mattress later. The sky looked a little dark. So, I covered Natalie's mattress with some beach towels, and we started the five-mile drive into town. Just a few blocks away from Spruce Street, we pulled up to a red light. When the first raindrops hit the windshield, we looked at each other. *Oh no! Turn green, turn green,* I prayed. Within seconds, the sky opened up. Water poured down as we waited for the light to change. There was nothing we could do, and the towels wouldn't help at all. Natalie's mattress would be soaked. As the rain beat down on the truck, I felt defeated.

Natalie said, "Mom, I don't care if my mattress is wet. It'll dry. I'm still glad we moved everything."

By the time we got the wet mattress into the house, it was getting late, so we picked up the boys on our way home. They were surprised when Natalie told them how we had packed bags for each of them and moved all their beds, blankets, and pillows to the new house.

"Did you move the TV or Xbox 360?" Ryan asked.

"No, we don't have cable yet," I said.

It was after 9:00 pm when Scott slowly walked into his parents' house. Everyone was in the kitchen, filling up their plates for dinner. He hadn't even closed the sliding glass door when the kids started asking about where we were sleeping that night. The boys were pleading to stay at Jim and Diane's so that they could still play their video games, and Natalie was begging to sleep at the new house.

Scott rubbed his head, looking confused. He sighed and looked at me. "What are they talking about?"

"When it stopped raining earlier, Natalie and I borrowed Les's truck and moved all of our bedding, pillows, and the kids' mattresses to the new house."

He looked at me in disbelief.

"The only thing we couldn't lift was our mattress and box spring," I said.

"I'm tired, and it's late."

"We kind of have to do it. No one has a pillow or blanket, and all our toothbrushes and clothes for the morning are there too."

Scott grabbed a plate to eat dinner while Natalie and I dried out the truck bed again. Getting our queen-size mattress set in the truck was no problem for Scott and me, but once we got to the new house it was a different story. A railing and a short landing made it difficult to get our box spring up to the second floor. When we finally flopped into bed that night, it was almost midnight. I was happy to finally be in our house. It felt comfortable.

"Happy anniversary," I said.

## *Struggling with an organizing project?*

- *Use music* – *Listening to your favorite songs will make tedious sorting seem less like a chore.*

- *Try the buddy system* – *Find a friend who also wants to clean out space. Having someone to share your successes and frustrations with along the way can be very helpful.*

- *Celebrate small victories* – *It can be overwhelming to do a large room. Break it down into sections. Make sure to cheer and pat yourself on the back as you accomplish each one.*

- *Plan a special event* – *What do you want to do when the project is complete? You could invite a friend over to show off the space and spend time together. If you have created a special reading or crafting room, allow yourself time to enjoy using the new area.*

# MAINTENANCE

Once a space is organized, you need to make a plan to maintain it. It's natural for your needs, goals, and interests to change. Think of evaluating your spaces and time as "taking inventory." It doesn't mean anything has to leave or change. You will just be aware of what you have and how you are spending your time.

Making a plan for how often you do this and a specific limit to how much you keep is key. If you live in an extremely large home, you may be able to have a whole room designated just for your shoe collection. Otherwise, you may make a rule that you can only have the number of shoes that will fit comfortably on your shoe rack, or for every pair of shoes you buy, an old pair must go. You create the rules. Rules you have created are easier to enforce than arbitrary ones.

# CHAPTER FIFTEEN

# *Be Open to the Possibilities*

Clearing the clutter makes space for new opportunities.

Beside our mattresses and a couple suitcases of clothes, our home was practically empty. There were no chairs to sit on or tables for lamps. The living room was filled with tools, a table saw, and stacks of new trim to be hung. For several days, we had no curtains on the windows, so we crouched down when we walked to and from the shower. Scott had moved our grill to the house earlier in the spring, so we ate outside at our card table with folding chairs. Living like this reminded me of when we went camping as a family. The daily activities we took for granted, like showering and cooking, were suddenly an adventure. *What foods could we eat without having any silverware or dishes? Did we pack any towels?*

The first thing I wanted to do in our new house was take a bath in my cast-iron tub. I was grateful my in-laws had welcomed us into their home, but there is a level of relaxation and letting down your guard that I believe you can only feel when you are in your own space. It's what makes you want to go home after being on vacation. It's that calm, comfortable feeling many of my clients strive for when organizing their spaces.

Everywhere I turned, there were things that needed to be done in our house; towel racks to hang, paint to scrape off windows, dusty shelves to wipe. For the first few days, I just wanted to spend time reconnecting with the kids. There were only two weeks left of summer before everyone would be back in school and I would have the house to myself. Projects could wait until then. One thing we did need to do right away though was get some furniture into the house. That weekend, Scott and I started moving chairs, tables, and lamps. The funniest sight was our brown leather couch in the living room right in front of the table saw and long piles of trim. With each piece of furniture we added, our house became more of a home.

The first day of school was a crisp, sunny morning. I took the annual pictures on the porch of our new house. Scott, Natalie, and Zach left at the same time, all headed to the high school, and Ryan and I walked down the road to his new bus stop. I smiled as he waved to me, and I stood on the sidewalk and watched his bus drive away.

I leisurely walked back to the quiet house. Everyone was gone, and I was completely alone. I had wanted to be home to take care of my family for such a long time, and now, it was happening. It was such a long road with a lot of stress, hard work, and faith along the way, but I was happy with how things were turning out. With our house situation under control, I could explore the new avenues and opportunities with my business.

I started speaking more to groups of people. A client asked me to speak to her moms and babies group. I was excited to talk with them because I know how young families get bombarded with kid's toys, school papers, and art work. The women with elementary-age children struggled to keep up with all the school papers that came home. They wanted to preserve their child's memories but found the bins they designated for keepsakes were quickly overflowing.

As a teacher, I remember one of the favorite classroom jobs was Paper Passer. There was always a large stack of papers to return, and the kids loved racing around the room, handing them out. Students left for the day with their backpacks stuffed, and their parents were on the receiving end of that full book bag.

I'm not sure it is possible to save every piece of artwork or paper your child has done nor is it advisable. One box per child is probably plenty. I encouraged the young moms to be selective when choosing what to preserve and, when old enough, include their children in the decision process. There are better options to keep these childhood treasures without needing to put an addition on their home. One great way is to have the memories transformed into a hardbound book for the parents and children to enjoy for years to come.

Following the speaking session with the moms, I had an interesting task present itself. A woman called and said her relative was in the hospital and needed help. She asked, "Could I hire you to clear out a hoarded house?"

In my mind, I answered, "No," but I agreed to meet her for a consultation. I told Scott about the conversation and that I wasn't going to take the job.

He was confused and said, "Why wouldn't you clear out a hoarded house?"

I said nervously, "I've never done it before."

"What do you mean you haven't done it before? You cleared out our house and loved doing it! Why wouldn't you do it for a client?"

He was right. I had done it for our house, but I was afraid to take on this new venture. There were so many unknowns. For starters, I didn't know how to charge someone for a whole house or even how to write a proposal for the job. Could I really do it?

I thought back to the first few weeks where I was sorting all the items in our new house. I remembered the excitement I felt working at the house and how I didn't want to leave. I decided I had to give it a try.

First, I had to figure out how to write up a proposal. I carefully selected the perfect words, making sure the grammar and punctuation were right. Scott had written contracts when he was building homes, so I asked him to look at it.

He smiled and said, "You have complete paragraphs and punctuation."

"I know. I checked," I said proudly

Scott said, "No, you shouldn't have complete sentences. Just a brief description of each service and the cost for it."

He patiently taught me how to figure out pricing and create a contract and spreadsheet. It was ironic how we had basically switched careers. It wasn't so long ago that I had been helping him as he first started writing lesson plans. Now, the tables were turned, and I was relying on his expertise for an organizing proposal.

A few weeks later, I was completely stunned one day, while I was sitting on my knees. sorting through items with a client. Her husband walked in and watched for a few minutes as we were deciding what to do with things from their attic and then quietly asked, "Would you be interested in doing an organizing session for TV?"

He worked for a local news channel, and they had a series called Focus on Families. They were interested in showing an organizing session in action. This would be great publicity for my business. It was up to me to find a family and determine a space to organize.

I chose to do a closet. Maximizing storage space is a problem that impacts most families. Whether their homes are 900 square feet or 5,000 square feet, everyone feels that they don't have enough room in their closets. My friend Kirsten was kind enough to offer her home. The closet in her master bedroom had a sloped ceiling, and like most older homes, there was very little storage space. Her main goals were to make it more functional and maximize the storage capability.

The next step was purging. Taking inventory of what you have and what you need are a big part of this process. So, we went through the clothes and shoes, and I asked Kirsten to evaluate each item. I asked her the most important question we can ask when cleaning out our clothes: "Do you love it?" If we don't like an item, then we probably won't wear it. Kirsten and I organized the clothes she decided to keep and put the others in boxes to donate and consign.

After we started the session, I was so engrossed in what we were doing that I forgot all about the microphone they had attached to me. The reporter and camera crew packed up after taping for three hours. I was eager to see the edited session that would air in a few weeks.

With all these new opportunities, my business was growing. It was several months before I took another waitressing shift. I needed to work periodically to remain on the part-time list. I found a day when I didn't have an organizing client scheduled and signed up for an event. I walked into the room and waited with the other servers to hear our assignments.

Someone muttered under their breath, "I didn't know she even worked here anymore."

One of the part-timers asked excitedly, "How's your business going? I saw you on TV!" I felt a sense of accomplishment. She was so excited and wanted to hear all the details. Inspired by my success, another coworker pulled me aside later and told me his aspirations for a different career.

I was grateful that waitressing had helped me through the tough financial times over the past few years, but I was on the other side now. It was such a relief to know I didn't have to depend on a job I didn't love anymore.

*Think about a pair of pants that doesn't fit right. When we see them in the closet, we pass over them, choosing something that fits better. Why? Because we invested time and money into them?*

- **Sale** – *The price should not be the determining factor for whether an item is bought or not. It doesn't matter if a sweater was bought at a great price if you don't like it.*

- **Paid a lot** – *Expensive clothes don't gain any value being kept in our closet.*

- **Consigning** – *Some money can be regained from taking good quality clothing to sell at a consignment shop. At least this way, it doesn't waste away in the closet.*

- **Tax deduction** – *Getting a tax deduction from clothes that are a little older is another way to recoup some of the cost.*

*Purging clothes that no longer fit our shape or style makes room for the clothing we love.*

*Don't you want more room in your closet for things you love?*

# CHAPTER SIXTEEN

# *Your Perception Matters*

Are you holding yourself back?

What are the limitations you have imposed on your level of success or happiness?

For a while, I wondered what might have happened if I had changed my career path earlier. What if I had quit when I had wanted to when Natalie was born? My life would have taken a whole different path. The path that my life had taken was not easy or the one I had envisioned, but I realized it was the path I needed to take. Just because I wanted to quit years before didn't mean I was truly ready for it to happen.

I look back with new eyes at the years I spent feeling unfulfilled in my first profession. What I once thought of as wasting time I now consider as a time of conserving energy. I needed stamina to carry me through the change. Maybe I needed to teach until I recognized the feeling that something was missing. The emptiness I felt in the classroom propelled me on this journey.

I have never been one to make big decisions quickly, so when I finally decided to change my career, I was certain that I had exhausted every possibility and teaching was not the career for me. I have never once regretted my choice. In fact, a few times a year, I still have nightmares where I am frustrated in a classroom. When I wake up, I am reassured that I made the right choice for my family and me.

All the years that I wanted to leave teaching to be home with my family, I had prayed to win the lottery or for something extraordinary to happen that allowed me to quit. Although winning the lottery would have been great, I am grateful that it didn't happen. If the opportunity to quit my job would have been handed to me so easily, there are so many character building lessons I would have missed. The scrutinizing eyes of others helped to build the courage I needed to change my life. I had to search deep inside myself for what I wanted and then swim against the stream to find my bliss. When times were financially tough, I learned to remain positive and focus on what was important. I was thankful each month when we could pay our bills and I didn't have to sell my plasma to do it. I was given an incredible chance to test myself and my faith. The struggles helped me live in the present and appreciate the simple things in life.

When I left my teaching career to start my own business, I wanted to be passionate about my job. I didn't want to pray for snow delays in the winter and count the days until the end of the year. My ultimate goal was to enjoy my life each day and season. If I was doing something where I felt happy and fulfilled, then I could be more present to spend quality time with my family.

Organizing is about much more than the physical things. It is actively, consciously creating your life. It is choosing to let go of both the physical and mental clutter that are getting in your way, the things that no longer fit who we are or want to be. Life throws new opportunities and challenges at us constantly. Organizing your life requires paying attention to your daily life. Sometimes I will recognize that I have taken on too much or am rushing through life. I find it much easier to say no and cut out the things that I don't need or love without worrying what others think of my choices.

When I began my business, the amount of time I spent organizing with clients was minimal. There were often days when I wasn't working. Looking back, I treated my business more like a hobby. My top concern was my quality of life. The goal had been happiness, not money. I loved spending time at home and was happy to be available when Scott and the kids called me to bring iPads, sneakers, and other forgotten items to school. I felt like I was making up for lost time with them.

Like a child getting taller each year, I didn't notice the steady growth that happened with my business.

One day, Ryan commented, "Healthier Spaces Organizing is a real business now."

"What do you mean it's a real business now?"

"Well, before we could call you from school and you were probably home, but now, you go to work every day like a real job," he said.

Ryan was right. Whether I was organizing with a client or attending a networking event, I was working on my business every day. Three years after I had made my first vision board, I decided it was time to create a new one to see what was on the horizon. This board was very different from the first one. I was no longer seeking what I wanted. I could see my new focus would be on building my company and making a sustainable career. It was about taking my business seriously, thinking bigger, and being in charge. For the first few years, I had been content to just be in my new career. Today, I still love my job, but I also want to grow my business and impact the lives of more people. I realized that I could share more of my ideas about organizing by writing a book and traveling to speak to people all over.

As I daily drove from client to client or to deliver donations, I was constantly aware of the time and often looked at the clock in my car. The elementary school schedule was still ingrained in my head. Students came in at 8:45 am, lunch was from 11:45 am to 12:45 pm, special classes were at 2:30 pm, and dismissal was at 3:30 pm.

One spring day, after an organizing session, I had two boxes and one large bag of unneeded school supplies my client wanted me to donate. It was 12:15 pm: lunchtime, the perfect time to take supplies to Leslie at school.

As I pulled up to the building, I felt like it was another lifetime from when I was a teacher, going there every day, counting down until the year was over. But, it was only four years before. It was surreal that I would be walking into school during the middle of the day and leaving after a half hour. I signed in at the office and put on a visitor's badge.

The secretaries were excited to see me. They asked, "How's your business going?"

"It's going great. I was invited by the school district to participate in the local business health fair, and I was just on TV."

They said, "You look so happy."

"Thank you. I am." I beamed as I walked down the hall, thinking of the differences between my jobs. I work longer hours now, sometimes even on weekends and holidays. I no longer had paid sick or personal days, or my summers off. But, I also didn't have migraines or cysts anymore. I wouldn't trade the happiness and satisfaction I felt on a daily basis with the security and stability of my former career. I was confident with the choices I had made to leave.

I rushed down the hall, eager to surprise Leslie.

A teacher stopped me in the hallway, excited to share how my decision to leave inspired her to make a change. She wasn't the only one to tell me this. Other people had confided in me that they were encouraged to make choices in their life because of my decision. When my resignation became official, my colleagues had questioned my health and sanity. What once seemed crazy ended up inspiring others to make a life change.

Leslie was surprised to see me and excited for all the puzzles, markers, and art supplies I had for her students. I was glad they could be used. As her students started filing in for the afternoon, I walked out the door and smiled as I joyously left the school.

> *"One day, you will wake up, and there won't be any more time to do the things you've always wanted. Do it now."*
>
> *-Paolo Coelho*

# *Epilogue*

It's difficult to believe that it was just five years ago when I said goodbye to teaching. The life I was striving for included a new career that I would love and flexibility to spend quality time with my family. I now have the passionate job that I was searching for, and my life has improved in more ways than I could have imagined. All three of the important things that I once wrote on my wish-list are now my priorities: Making memories with my family, spending time with friends, and focusing on my health.

The road was not easy but worth every bit of struggle. I worried so much about how my need to change would affect my family. I didn't want it to affect them at all, but it did have an impact—it transformed our family life for the better. More than anything else I have achieved, I showed my children to follow their hearts and strive for happiness.

When Scott decided to support me, he knew it was a risk to sell our house, leave my job, and start a new career. There was no way to predict the future and how things would turn out. In the tough times when our house wasn't selling, when we didn't have the money to go out to eat or I only had a handful of jobs in a month, he never said a word. During the tough times, his action of standing by me and supporting my dream spoke loud and clear. It was his unwavering devotion that made the change possible. The journey served to deepen our relationship.

Natalie is finishing her college degree, majoring in international relations. She is again overseas for a year; this time in Africa. At the end of May, I flew to visit her in Senegal. We spent two weeks traveling and connecting. I thought often during my time there how the trip would not have been possible at the end of a school year if I had still been in the classroom.

In high school, Zach suffered from undiagnosed lower back pain for nearly two years. With my flexible schedule, I was able to take him to over a dozen professionals to find that juvenile arthritis was the cause and get him treatment. He started college in the fall and I was fortunate to be able to arrange my schedule so I could drive him up and get him settled in.

When we first moved to Spruce Street, Ryan was in elementary school and missed being with his friends. He didn't know anyone that lived close to our new home. After a year, he met kids and has enjoyed walking and riding his bike all around town. He goes to the park and fishing with friends. Ryan started his freshman year of high school, and I'm so appreciative that I will be fully present to enjoy his final years at home with us, I know they will go by quickly.

My mom has commented on several occasions how fortunate it is that I am no longer teaching. Despite what I thought about my kids being too old to need me, there have been many important times that I have been able to be there for them in ways that stretched beyond just my time. Because I've been more fulfilled and happier in my life, I'm able to give out more positive energy to everyone in my life, including strangers. It really is true what they say about filling up your cup first—you have more of yourself to give to others.

Scott has been teaching in our school district for a few years. First, he had a teaching position at the high school and the last two years he has been in 5th grade. He decided to resign from coaching football. Scott and I have had time to spend together, enjoying our home, and new life with only one child at home. This journey has served to deepen our relationship.

As we continued to make improvements in our home, neighbors commented how much they love what we are doing. We were asked by the historical society to include our home on a tour of homes, because people were interested in seeing the changes we had done. I continue to be passionate about recycling and repurposing items to eliminate waste. A few years ago, I adopted a highway, clearing trash from the roadside. I am currently planning an Organize Your Life county-wide recycling event that will be held annually.

The Lazy Girl book club went away for the weekend this spring. One night we decided to make vision boards, and I was excited to see how mine would turn out this time. The phrase I decided to put at the top said, "Time to Shine." Other words that caught my attention were "Travel, Wildest Dreams, and Get Ready to Take on the World".

As I speak in front of growing audiences about the changes I made in my life and inspire others to clear the clutter in their homes, it's been amazing to see how even the smallest choices we make in our own lives can have the power to impact the futures of so many. The struggle I faced with a having a job that drained me along with the feeling that life was passing me by, is an unbalance I think a lot of people experience and is often mis-labeled under the name Mid-Life Crisis. It's not so much a crisis as it is an awareness that comes with age. We're all searching for meaning and purpose, and sometimes all that's needed to find it is a little courage to create a healthier space.

# RESOURCES

# *Book Club Questions*

Do you want to share *Organizing Her Life* with your book club? Here are some conversational questions about the book directly from the author, Laura Souders. To schedule an exclusive skype with your book club or to hire Laura for a speaking engagement in your area, visit HealthierSpaces.com

1. In the book, Laura talks about feeling drained and needing to fill her spirit. What fills your spirit? What drains it?

2. What is your favorite organizing tip from book?

3. What are you most motivated to change in your space or in your life after reading the book?

4. Laura's choices in the book went against what everyone thought she should do. A motivational speech she gives is called "Cutting out the Shoulds in Your Life". What have you done in the past that went against what others thought you *should* do?

5. *"Organize your life now, so you don't look back in five years and realize chaos and clutter planned your life for you."* Five years seems like a long time, but it goes by quickly and the time will pass anyway. Where do you want to be in five years?

## *Top 3 Important Things In Your Life*

What are the top 3 things you consider to be most important in your life? Write them below.

1.

2.

3.

Now think about the areas in your life where you spend the most time and energy. List them.

1.

2.

3.

- How do your important things match up with where you actually spend your time and energy?

- Allowing something to take up your space that really doesn't serve you, means there is less time and space for things that bring you joy.

# *How to Create a Vision Board*

- Gather the supplies you will need:
  - A variety of old magazines
  - Glue
  - Scissors
  - Poster board
  - Markers

- Start by looking through the magazines and ripping out any page you like. You may be drawn to a picture, quote, colors, or a feeling you get from a page.

- Don't judge what you tear out at this stage.

- Once you have a pile of magazine pages, begin to trim around each one nicely.

- It's time to analyze your pictures. Lay them all out. What do you notice? What is the message you see?

- Arrange the pieces on the poster board, then glue them down.

- Write any additional words or phrases to make your vision board complete, using the markers.

# *How to Make Your Own Quote Book*

- Search Pinterest or magazines to find quotes that motivate you, empower you, or bring you joy.

- "Pin" the quotes on a virtual board or print and cut them out.

- Quotes can be arranged on thick paper to display, arranged in an album or put on a bulletin board.

- Use the quotes to inspire you or help you get through tough times.

### Quotes from *Organizing Her Life*

*"Organizing is about the stuff, but it is about much more than the physical things. It is actively, consciously creating your life."*

*"There is no need to feel guilty about change"*

*"Organize your life now so you don't look back in five years and realize chaos and clutter planned your life for you."*

*"It all begins with a plan. Make a plan to get started."*

*"Letting go of things you don't need, bring the exact things you do need into your life."*

# *Making an Effective To Do List*

- I use a sheet of paper and visually separate it into thirds. The first section is for things that are *Urgent* to complete. The next section contains tasks that need done *Soon*, but not immediately. The last section, *Later*, has projects that are on my radar but are more long range.

- Look at a calendar for reminders about upcoming obligations.

- Using verbs, briefly state what you need to do. For example: Find passport, mail bills, buy groceries. Each item has their own line and if there is more than one part to the task, they are listed below the item.

- Use a checkmark to cross things off or give yourself a star when you finish an item.

- When choosing to carry out the tasks, estimate how much time each will take. Plan to sandwich smaller tasks between larger ones.

- Don't make your list too long, it will get overwhelming and you will be discouraged when it seems that you haven't completed very much.

# *Income Versus Expenses*

How much do you need to make each month?
If you are considering switching careers, you need to know the bottom line.

First- List all sources of income.
Next- List all the monthly expenses, be sure to include:

- Housing costs- Rent or mortgage
- Phone, cable, internet
- Utilities- Electric- Energy- Water- Trash
- Car Payments and Loans
- Insurance for Auto, Home, and Health (Divide to find out what you would pay a month)
- Memberships and Subscriptions (like the gym and magazines)
- Groceries and eating out
- Gas
- Clothing
- Miscellaneous expenses like haircuts

*Take an average of the last few months, err on the high side, to be safe.

Last- Add all up to find your total expenses and compare it to the money you have coming in each month. Take into account money that you have in savings accounts, before making your decision.

# *Unique Ideas to Pass Along Unloved Items*

Everyone wants to pass their unneeded items to someone who will appreciate them. Below are some creative suggestions to give them to a new home.

o Charity Raffle Basket- Start by using gifts you have been given that are not your taste or style. It's best to use new items that are still in their original packaging. Plan a theme around that item. For instance, if you had a mug to use, then you could add some hot cocoa and maybe a nice journal to create a "Snowy Day" basket.

o Swap- You could create "Swap Parties" with friends and family. There are so many things you can swap, but the basic idea is the same. They work well with children and adults.

o Books- Have all participants bring books, from one to several. Keep track of how many books each person donated and the total number of books. If there are 20 books, write one number for each book on a different ticket. Put the tickets in a bowl. Without looking, each person picks as many tickets as the number of books they brought, and the number they draw denotes their order from which they choose books.

o Jewelry swap- Have costume jewelry you don't wear? Wouldn't it be nice to trade it for something more your style?

o Household decorations- Just because our decorating taste has changed, doesn't mean someone else won't like it.

- Kitchen Gadgets- Some culinary tools sound great, but once you get them home, you really don't use them much. Maybe someone else would find it more helpful.
- Clothing- Remember how fun it was to switch clothes with your friends when you were a teenager? It still can be. Create a swap party with friends or for children's clothing.

*If some people bring more items than they care to select, you can donate the extra things.

## *Donation Resources*

Search first in your local area. Below are some that have nationwide locations.

**Donationtown.org-** enter your zip code to schedule a pick up for items like books, clothing, and appliances.

**Pickupplease.org-** books, clothing, household, and furniture small enough for one person to lift, benefits US Veterans.

**Salvationarmyusa.org-** books, clothing, household goods.

***

## *Recycling Resources*

**Earth911.com-** Enter your zip code and item you want to recycle for local options.

**Gazelle**.com- a site that recycles smart phones and other devices.

**Lancastercreativereuse.**org/directory-creative-reuse-centers.html – an option for recycling art materials.

National Association of
**Productivity & Organizing**
——— Professionals ———

Education. Research. Strategies.

# *Bio*

Laura Souders, owner of Healthier Spaces Organizing, helps people clear the clutter from their lives by uniquely organizing each space to fit her client's needs with creative solutions. She is a Professional member of the National Association for Productivity and Organizing Professionals (NAPO), the Environmental Special Interest Group, and she holds certificates in Chronic Disorganization and Basic Hoarding from the Institute for Challenging Disorganization (ICD). She's a board member of Central Penn Networking Group, a mentor for the Central Pennsylvania Association of Female Executives, and a traveling speaker—inspiring others to transform their lives one space and one day at a time.

# *Connect with Me*

Need to hire a speaker for your next event? Need organizing help?  Contact me through my website www.healthierspaces.com . You can also sign up for my newsletter to get more organizing tips.

Planning a recycling and donation event in Dauphin County, Pennsylvania in the Fall of 2019. If you would like to be a part of it, please email me at laurasouders@msn.com

See before and after pictures of spaces I organize, along with event updates by liking my Facebook page, Healthier Spaces Organizing.

Did you enjoy reading Organizing Her Life? I'd love to see your review on Amazon or Goodreads!"

# *Acknowledgements*

There are so many people I want to thank for helping me along my journey. First and most importantly, my husband, **Scott**. You have been instrumental in the creation of this book. Thank you for understanding the long hours I spent typing away on my laptop, being my technology guy, and participating in competitive puzzling with me when I needed a break. You don't say much, but when you do, it's worth the wait, especially during our brainstorming sessions. The way our relationship grows continues to astonish me.

**Natalie**- you were the first one to encourage me to write this book, believing in me and the story. My path has led me to exactly where I wanted to be, able to be by your side, available for you, **Zach** and **Ryan**.

**Tessa**- for truly bringing my book to life. Without you, the ideas and pages of Organizing Her Life would still be locked on the screen of my laptop. Your positive energy made the process a wonderful journey. Book Doula is the perfect title for you!

My sister, **Les**- on our long walks together you always help me put things in perspective. I love how we make each other laugh, the big, silent shoulder-shake type of laugh.

**Becky**- for gently guiding me along my path. Your vision and insight have been invaluable to me.

My teaching friend **Leslie**- you helped me through some of the toughest days, crying with me, reminding me why I was doing it, and cheering me on.

**Rhonda**- for teaching me how to pray and turn to God for guidance. You helped me see that His plan for me would be bigger than my plan, if I just let go.

**Kirsten**- I will forever be thankful for your brainstorming that created the brand Healthier Spaces. Thank you for giving me the spark I needed to fulfill my dreams.

**My parents**- you have always wanted the best for me. You gave me the foundation to believe I could achieve anything I wanted if I worked hard. I am appreciative for the drive and ambition you instilled in me.

**Jim and Diane**- Thank you for welcoming us into your home and helping us in so many ways to make our life transformation possible.

**The Angry Plasterer and Brad**- Thank you for the time and love you put into creating our home.

**My best friend**- for your pure honesty. You laid out the plan I needed and believed in me. Thank you for helping me to discover my dreams and find the courage to follow them. I will always be grateful for our friendship.

**Linda**- You are such a supportive friend and I look forward to your weekly check-ins. Thank you for being my trash picking companion.

My first readers- **Bobbi**, **Nadine**, **Kristi**, and **Nancy**, for your invaluable feedback that guided my writing.

97730553R00139

Made in the USA
Middletown, DE
06 November 2018